Step Out of the Box with a Bang!

A Rapid-Read Handbook™ from
breakthroughskills.com

Step Out of the Box with a Bang!

THE POSITIVE, PROACTIVE, AND EXCUSE-FREE WORK LIFE

Doug Davin and Diana Morris

New Heights Media, Inc.
The People Skills Experts™
Fort Lee, NJ

Published by New Heights Media, Inc.
260 Columbia Avenue, Suite 5, Fort Lee, NJ 07024
Toll Free: 877-312-5400
Phone: 201-224-3800
Fax: 201-224-6688
E-mail: info@breakthroughskills.com
www.breakthroughskills.com

Publisher's Cataloging-in-Publication Data
Davin, Doug.

Step out of the box with a bang! : the positive, proactive, and excuse-free work life / Doug Davin and Diana Morris. — Fort Lee, N.J. : New Heights Media,Inc., 2009.

p. ; cm.

ISBN: 978-1-891019-26-5

1. Conflict management. 2. Job stress. I. Morris, Diana. II. Title.

HD42 .D386 2009
658.4053-dc22   2008925953

Project coordination by Jenkins Group, Inc.
www.BookPublishing.com
Cover design by Chris Rhoads
Interior design by Diane Neumeister

Printed in the United States of America
13 12 11 10 09 • 5 4 3 2 1

*"*No pessimist ever discovered the secret of the stars, or sailed to an uncharted land, or opened a new doorway for the human spirit.*"*

—Helen Keller
Humanitarian, author, and
advocate for the deaf and blind

Step Out of the Box with a Bang!

THE POSITIVE, PROACTIVE, AND EXCUSE-FREE WORK LIFE

CONTENTS

Success. . .Multiplied

Breakthroughskills.com is a professional self-improvement community and webstore. Our original resources—Rapid-Read Handbooks™, BTS QuickTools™, Breakthrough Coaching, Workshops, and Telesession calls—zero-in on seven Breakthrough Skills essential for reaching the highest levels of success in your work:

1. **Conflict Management:** *Keep cool in hot situations*

2. **Confident Communication:** *Sharpen your writing and presentations*

3. **Active Listening:** *Hear the possibilities*

4. **High Possibility Thinking:** *Set great expectations*

5. **Leadership and Teambuilding:** *Unify and motivate your team*

6. **Practical Persuasion:** *Create the win-win*

7. **Skillful Self Promotion:** *Boost your reputation for excellence*

We're Doug Davin and Diana Morris, and for the last 25 years, we've been helping people at some of the world's largest companies reach new heights of success.

You know you've got a great future ahead of you. We know it too, and we're serious about helping you.

Start building your breakthrough today.

BREAKTHROUGH
skills.com

Make This Book Your Own

Each of us comes to a book like this at different points. We've got unique talents and goals. Our experiences vary widely. We work in different fields. We know different people.

So make this book your own by reading with a critical eye. Choose the ideas that make the most sense for you and adapt them for your career or business.

Then break through to new heights of success by zeroing in on these ideas and putting them in motion with everything you've got.

Breakaway Café

Make yourself a cup of something delicious, sharpen a pencil, and get ready to remind yourself of how talented and valuable you are...

Think of a time...

Remember a time when you felt positive and excited about work. Maybe it was when you worked for a leader who had a gift for getting everyone fired up about the future. Or at an event where the energy level was so high that people left feeling excited and alive, ready to take on any challenge. Maybe it was that time you felt the thrill of finally seeing a dream come true. Even something as ordinary as a lunch with friends may have given you fresh ideas for moving in new directions at work.

Build on this success...

1. What was the situation? Who else was involved? What created the positive energy? What was your contribution?

2. When did you realize something extraordinary had happened?

3. How did the positive energy affect you afterward?

4. What two or three steps can you take to generate this kind of positive energy in the future?

Let's Go!

Remember being a kid? Running, jumping, yelling, flying down the sidewalk on your bike? Freedom! The world was your oyster. Everything was ahead of you and there was nothing you couldn't create, achieve, fix, or invent. Whether you were outgoing or laid back, you were filled with positive expectation about the future because it was all out there, just waiting for you.

> "Afoot and lighthearted.
> I take to the open road,
> Healthy, free, the world before me,
> The long brown path before me,
> Leading wherever I choose."
>
> — Walt Whitman, American poet
> "Song of the Open Road"

What if we told you that you could feel this way about your work today—only better? Because now, you have perspective, maturity, and resources. And because now you have past successes that are proof of your talents and potential. So you can have the joys and hopes and high expectations you had back then, plus the confidence that you've got what it takes to turn them into reality.

And what if we told you that achieving this is not only simple, it's also a lot easier than the alternative: seeing work as a drudge that you resign yourself to because, well, *sigh* you have to pay the bills?

In your brand new business head and heart, you go to work expectant and wide-eyed. The pressures you feel, the disappointments, your worries and mis-steps…all these fade to the back of your mind, and you're left with faith in yourself and in the people you work with. Your mind is fresh, full of possibilities and new hope. Your dreams have kicked up a notch. And they all seem within reach.

Does this sound impossible? Or maybe just a lot of "happy talk"? It isn't. We've seen High Possibility Thinking, the Breakthrough Skill you're about to learn, create seismic shifts in people, teams, and even whole companies. A few years ago, we watched one company's senior leaders shuffle into a meeting room, eyes downcast, looking defeated and saying things like, "All I need is one job offer, and I'm out of here tomorrow. You know what? Make that today," and "This company has no life left." One year later, the very same people were telling us things like, "I wouldn't work for any other business in this industry. This is the best company," "We just don't talk in negative terms any more," and "This is the greatest place to work."

What happened? All we did was give these leaders a taste of High Possibility Thinking, and they never wanted to go back. They cleared their minds of "can't" and took their company from five consecutive years of losses to 18 percent profit in one year. We asked them when things started to change, when the company went from get-me-outta-here awful to "the greatest place to work," and they gave us the title of this book with their answer: "It was right after last year's meeting. We finally stepped out of the box of our own negativity and defeat. The business changes took time, but <u>we</u> changed right away."

Step Out of the Box with a Bang! is our first resource on the life-changing topic of High Possibility

Thinking. Inside, you'll find three sections filled with encouragement and our practical, use-them-now tips for building this vital Breakthrough Skill:

Positive Power:	Expect (and get) the best from people and situations
Proactive Power:	Anticipate success with deliberate action
Excuse-free Power:	Move into the future confident and solution oriented

We've also given you our signature **Working Wisdom** and **Leader Points,** proven ideas from our years of helping clients create their own personal, team, and business breakthroughs. As always, client names have been changed to protect their privacy, and some stories are composites we've created for the sake of brevity.

When you chose this book, you made a critical decision about how you intend to work and live: "I will find or create the positive potential in every situation. I expect to be discouraged from time to time, but I refuse to stay that way." The title itself acknowledges that things won't always be perfect: you need to be *positive* in spite of setbacks, *proactive* to prevent problems, and *excuse-free* so people know they can count on you to make good things happen even when the going gets tough.

Business people who operate this way see fresh solutions and new possibilities where others see only problems. Leaders and managers who treat their teams this way end up with employees who go way beyond their expectations and become their champions: flexible, creative, and willing to run through walls for them. Business owners who run their companies this way find opportunities everywhere, spin gold out of rough spots, attract star performers, and build lasting customer relationships.

A promise

One of the timeless laws of business seems to be that real professionals with serious aspirations don't let anyone peek behind the curtain of their carefully managed image and see them angry or frustrated by challenges or crises. And that's a positive—it's great to have a reputation for being solid and consistent. But you don't want to have to earn that reputation by hiding behind that curtain, pretending to ignore setbacks, slapping on a happy face and smiling sweetly all the time, or by faking excitement over every mediocre idea. Not only is this exhausting and dismissive of your own genuine ideas and reactions, it can seem insincere, sometimes even insensitive, and get you written off as someone who doesn't assess situations in an honest, balanced way.

As always, our clients ground us. "How am I supposed to grit my teeth and say, 'No problem,' when it _is_ one?" they challenge, "or 'Sure thing,' when it _isn't_ one, without feeling like a phony?"

Fair enough.

So here's our promise: we will show you how you can build your High Possibility Thinking skills, not by having you join the local chapter of the Happy Smilers

Step Out of the Box with a Bang! • A Rapid-Read Handbook™

Club or delivering an Academy Award-worthy performance every day, but by actually being more honest and authentic than ever.

Begin to use our suggestions, and you'll be able to come out from behind the curtain and stay there, with nothing to hide and definitely nothing to fake. You'll be yourself, not "on" at work. With a head clear of pessimism and negative clutter, you'll relax and see clearly that every business situation—even the inevitable hiccups and calamities—has a thread of possibility, something positive you can build on. At least one thing went right. You learned a powerful lesson. A failure tested your guts. Rejection strengthened you. Or maybe you found out that you can't actually die of embarrassment.

Best of all, you'll have more energy for the good stuff: good meetings, great brainstorming sessions, stronger relationships, better ideas and more time to go after them.

We don't want you to waste one day—not one hour—on thinking that saps your energy and is anything less than soar-to-new-heights inspiring. Put this powerful asset in your breakthrough portfolio starting right now.

If you have questions or would like help with any part of *Step Out of the Box with a Bang!* send an email to info@breakthroughskills.com.

We'd love to hear from you.

—Doug and Diana

Part 1: Positive Power

Expect (and Get) the Best from People and Situations

It should have been a short and easy hike in New York's Catskill Mountains, but somehow we got lost. The trail (or what we thought was the trail) kept looping us further up the mountain instead of down. Tree after tree, rock after rock, we walked and walked. As the afternoon wore on, clouds started to gather. You can just imagine the sniping and griping that went on between us as the hours passed.

> "Clear your mind of can't."
>
> — Samuel Johnson,
> English writer and critic

The sun began to set. The rain arrived, and still we were lost. We made one last attempt to find the right trail back to the car, this time walking faster past the same trees and slipping over the same rocks. Once again, the path took us up instead of down, and once again we ended up arguing at the same spot. It seemed hopeless, and we were tired, muddy and hungry.

With no camping gear, we started looking for a dry spot on the ground to spend the night. As we gathered leaves and whatever else we could find to make a bed, we heard a dog barking, then voices. A group of hikers was passing through. We quickly told them about our predicament, walked with them for half an hour, then finally got our bearings and saw the way out.

A quick thanks, and we took to the trail ahead of them practically in a sprint. It was dark by the time we reached the car. We threw our packs in the trunk, got in, and spoke not one word to each other the entire trip home.

In talking about it later, we remembered feeling disoriented and frustrated, but also exposed and really vulnerable. Next time, we decided no matter how short the hike, we bring a compass and a map.

When we started to plan a book on High Possibility Thinking and positive expectation, for some reason we kept thinking about that afternoon in the Catskills and the anxiety of being exposed, unprotected from the elements. Why? Because being unprepared in the mountains was physically dangerous, but being unprepared at work for the daily assaults on your plans and dreams is just as dangerous in a different way.

We're talking about the program you deeply believe in that fizzles or flops, the leader you admire who falls from grace, bosses and clients who make promises they don't keep, promotions you deserve but don't get, colleagues who don't bother to say "Thanks" when they truly should, coworkers who take credit for your work, suppliers who break your trust when they underperform and overcharge, bread-and-butter clients who suddenly stop calling.

No matter how strong you are, these experiences can stretch your optimism to the breaking point, until one day, it simply snaps. The failed programs and fallen leaders, the disappointments and frustrations take their toll, and we've seen incredibly talented and valuable people become so discouraged that they begin to say things like, "Yeah, well, that's just the way it is around here," "Why bother? Nothing ever changes," and "Doesn't matter how hard you work. You're either one of the 'chosen,' or you're not."

But <u>you</u> won't be one of them. Because in this section, we gear up. Your equipment: positive expectation—the skill to see possibilities where others see only problems. To envision and then actively create an outcome that can actually be more favorable and higher potential than if the problem had never occurred in the first place. "I know it's silly," a good friend confided recently, "but I've always believed in making lemonade from the lemons I get handed. Besides, I happen to like lemonade, especially when I make it." Yeah, we get that.

Simply irresistible

Our friend isn't alone. In a recent Breakthrough Buzz survey, we asked professionals and business owners to tell us about the people skills that have helped them most in their careers. Seventy-three percent—nearly three quarters—of the 250 people who responded rated High Possibility Thinking as the skill most essential to anyone's success, and 78 percent said that having a positive attitude was the skill that had personally helped them most in their careers.

In fact, a growing body of research is producing evidence that positive emotions, thoughts, and questions are directly related to success at work and in school, plus long-term health, authentic happiness, creativity, and even problem-solving ability.

In universities, a movement called Positive Psychology, led by Martin Seligman, former President of the American Psychological Association and Professor of Psychology at the University of Pennsylvania, has been increasing the awareness of optimism's value and importance.

An article in the March 10, 2006 issue of the *Boston Globe* reported that Harvard University's Positive Psychology course, which emphasizes creating "a fulfilling and nourishing life" is among the university's most popular classes, with an enrollment of 855 students. And Harvard has some company. Positive Psychology courses are being taught on more than 100 campuses at colleges and universities around the country.

In the workplace, a process called Appreciative Inquiry, pioneered by David Cooperrider and Suresh Srivasta, both professors at Cleveland's Case Western University, has proven many times (for the likes of the US Navy, McDonalds, Avon Mexico, Hunter Douglas, and others) to strengthen teams, build individual confidence, get past significant obstacles, and make everyone more productive. In the *Encyclopedia of Positive Questions* (Lakeshore Communications, 2001) which Cooperrider wrote with Diana Whitney, Amanda Trosten-Bloom, and Brian S. Kaplin, the authors explain, "The practice of asking positive questions not only brings out the best in people and organizations, it also amplifies and magnifies the most positive, life-giving possibilities for the future."

John Powell's book *Happiness is an Inside Job* (Thomas More Association, 1989) summarizes the author's research on the lives and thinking styles of 100 of the most successful and happy people he could find. Powell's research team was confused because at first, they couldn't find a common denominator such as education, socioeconomic background, or profession among the people included in the study. Finally, though, they did uncover a common trait. As Powell explains, each person had the ability "to look for and find what is good in him or herself, in others and in all the situations in life."

In the Preface to Powell's book, Cooperrider explains, "The word 'goodfinder' had to be invented to describe this common trait. Because of their never-ending search for the positive—the good, the better, and the possible—and their ability to see and amplify the best in people and situations around them, these leaders were successful. Strengths were elevated. Weaknesses became irrelevant. And nothing about the leadership was Pollyannaish. They were experts at deliberately noticing, anticipating, and magnifying positive potential."

Maybe more amazing than its ability to create success is positive expectation's apparent link to health and longevity. An article on the growing popularity of Positive Psychology appeared in the January 7, 2007 *New York Times Sunday Magazine*. The author, D.T. Max, cited a University of Kentucky study in which researchers analyzed essays written by novices entering the School Sisters of Notre Dame. When the essays were compared to the nuns' lifespans, 9 out of 10 of the most positive nuns were still alive at 85, while only one in three of the least positive were still alive. More broadly, researchers concluded that positive emotions seemed to produce a 10-year increase in lifespan, more than the difference between nonsmokers and smokers.

My brain, my rules

The positive expectation these researchers are so passionate about is a skill more certain to help you create your next career or business breakthrough than any educational degree or type of work experience. It's a way of working built on the determination to create work you love or a business of your own design, rather than have one dropped on you by circumstances.

When you master the skill of positive expectation—the belief that not only is a positive outcome possible, it's simply a matter of time before your actions bring it about—you become invincible. Let the negative daily onslaught advance! Nothing it can serve up will be able to knock you off course. Disappointments will begin to look more like second chances ("We can learn something worthwhile from this"), and the glass will suddenly seem half full ("We didn't get the account, but we wrote a great proposal we can use with the next prospect"). You'll take a pass at being offended and instead strengthen a relationship by giving someone the benefit of the doubt ("John's usually so level-headed. This angry reaction is unusual for him"). You'll find yourself expecting—and getting—the best from people ("Bill's team will definitely make this work," "I have complete faith in Donna's project management skills"), and overlooking mistakes to dwell on someone's strengths ("We didn't make the deadline because of the error, but Susan's got an incredible eye for detail. I'm so relieved she found the mistake.").

You'll also see that you don't need a calamity to put positive expectation to work. In fact, optimism is at its most powerful as a proactive strategy you use every day, when your general attitude is consistently hopeful in genuine anticipation of good things to come, and your self-talk deliberately amps up opportunities and shushes obstacles…and we do mean *shushes*. When the temptation to give in to "I can't/don't/wouldn't/shouldn't…" arises, you say, out loud if you have to: "Shhh!…

…I am *not* going there."

…I've already decided to change my approach. I don't need to rethink that decision, and I'm not going to give up."

…that's just a bunch of negative nonsense. It's just as likely that things will work out if I apply myself."

…I'm working on that. It won't change overnight, but I'll get there."

The late Beverly Sills, perhaps the best-known American opera singer of the 1960s and 70s, earned the nickname Bubbles for her effervescent personality and positive outlook. Despite a life of personal pain, a deep vein of cheerfulness ran through every interview she gave and book she wrote that told you she wasn't successful in spite of her hardships, or even because of them. She was successful because she refused to let them control and define her life.

"A primary function of art and thought," she once said, "is to liberate the individual from the tyranny of his culture…and to permit him to stand beyond it in an autonomy of perception and judgment." *An autonomy of perception and judgment.* What a freeing thought! My brain, my rules. I decide what I expect, plan, say…and ultimately what I achieve.

Now *that's* a decision

What is it about positive people? They're like success magnets. They always seem to be in the right place when the plum assignment or opportunity arises. When they're not around, people talk about them in only the most flattering ways. Loyal friends and supportive coworkers surround them.

Working Wisdom

Vitamin O

Positive expectation is a timeless secret for mental, emotional, and even physical stamina. Think about the Apollo 13 ground crew for whom failure was "not an option."

Or Soichiro Honda whose determination to build what is today one of the world's largest car companies was tested not once, but five times through bombings, supply shortages, and even an earthquake.

Or Thomas Edison, the man who literally enlightened the world saying of his many failed attempts to invent the light bulb, "I haven't failed. I've found 1,000 ways that don't work."

In these and countless other stories, optimism—not just the belief that a positive outcome was possible, but the expectation that one was just around the corner—provided the mental, emotional, and even physical strength to stay the course until the dream became reality.

When they make a mistake, even the people who bear the brunt of it are forgiving. And no matter what they ask for, you just want to say, "Sure thing!"

It would be great if we were all born positive success magnets, but the truth is most of us aren't. We see the glass half empty. We replay the one mistake we made in the interview and forget the 20 things we did right. We focus on how far we still have to go to reach a goal instead of how far we've already come.

But this can change. If you weren't born with a naturally sunny outlook, you can develop one. And it's not difficult, though it does take determination to break some old habits and replace them with new ones. You start with the life-changing decision to stop letting yourself be bossed around by your feelings. Because while developing a more positive outlook isn't difficult, it is impossible if you run feelings-first into every situation.

Feelings are like the worst manager you could ever have: indecisive, unpredictable, unreliable, and flighty. Will it be a good day or a bad day? Depends on how he feels. On Monday, he's psyched about the week ahead. By Wednesday, after a few mishaps and frustrations, he blows up. Will he like your work? Depends on his mood. Will he give you the answers you need to finish the project due this week? Maybe…if he feels like it.

Sounds like a nightmare job, and it is. But if you're letting yourself be bossed around by your own feelings, you're actually working at this job. Your feelings will take you way up on Monday, and maybe way down on Tuesday. You'll react positively on Wednesday to an idea because it feels right, and then on Thursday the same idea will seem unworkable, and you'll wish you never agreed to try it. On Friday, you'll sign up for an expensive course that sounds exciting, but when the day comes, you won't show up for it because you don't feel like going. You'll fret for weeks about a meeting you dread but can't avoid. You'll be derailed for months by harsh criticism that you just can't get over.

Up. Down. Up down. Up up. Down down down.

Enough!

Jump off this rollercoaster. Stop asking your anger, embarrassment, fear, and goose bumps for advice and decide instead that you will respond to the people and pressures in your work life by expecting the best. Now, you're free and fully in charge. You can choose to be hopeful and upbeat even when…

> you just lost your job
>> the project was cancelled
>>> the client left
>>>> your sales are sliding
>>>>> your idea got shot down

...because even though you don't _feel_ optimistic, you can still _be_ optimistic. Some examples:

When...	If your goal is to...	Instead of...	You can choose to...
[Setback occurs]	[Achieve the breakthrough you're after]	[Reacting emotionally]	[Make conscious decisions based on optimism and positive expectation]
You lose a sale you worked on for six months to a competitor.	Develop this type of clientele as a steady source of business.	Allowing yourself to think, "If I can't close a sale after working on it for six months, I'm never going to tap this market."	"I believe I can excel in this high potential market. I learned a lot through from this experience. To find out more about this market, I will..."
A recruiter questions a six-month gap on your resume and then never calls you again.	Get the job of your dreams.	Freezing up and thinking, "I'll never find a better job because I lost so much time between jobs."	"I won't let this be an issue. I'll develop a quality answer to this question ('I was freelancing, taking a course to improve a skill, raising children, caring for a parent, regrouping and thinking about the type of job I truly want, which is why I'm so very interested in this job...')."
A senior leader or client tells you in the middle of your presentation to a room full of people that you've highlighted the wrong information.	Be promoted into a leadership position with a team of direct reports and P&L responsibility.	Thinking, "Well, there goes my future."	"I'm glad I didn't waste too much of the group's time. Now I know what they truly need to know. Because of this tough experience, I have lots of motivation to do an excellent job on my next presentation for them."

Pay attention to your confidence level when you deliberately choose to be optimistic in a tough situation. You'll notice that it shoots up instantly because any time you make a positive choice—any time you free yourself from the tyranny of your feelings, take control and steer your career or business in the direction you choose—you exercise real power. You may not be able to control the circumstances, but do you ever command the result.

A good friend of ours once worked for an international chocolate company where teeming bowls of mouth-watering candy sat on almost every horizontal surface in the building. We met when her company became one of our clients. One day, as we sat in the conference room chowing down on the free chocolate, we noticed she never touched it. Not one delicious, velvety morsel. Ever. Why? It seemed like a such a wonderful perk to us—free candy, c'mon! "I decided when I took this job that I would never touch the candy," she said. "And I never have. We all joke about our company version of the college freshman 10. Only we're all older than that, so in our case it's more like the freshman 15. I knew if I started eating candy, I'd regret it, so it was better to just not even go there." And even though she worked there for six years, she never so much as touched the free candy—not even at the holiday parties. Now *that's* a quality decision. Clear. Simple. Once and done. A decision made for the right reasons.

Challenge yourself to make a once-and-done quality decision to stop consulting your feelings when the going gets rough. Instead, deliberately choose optimism and positive expectation. Clear. Simple. Once and done. A decision that will change your life.

Working Wisdom

Flawed, fickle, and fleeting

For years, "trust your feelings" and "do what your heart tells you" were popular pieces of advice given to us by well-meaning friends and colleagues, and it was good advice—to a point. Feelings can play a role in decision-making, prompting you to look further into an idea that feels right or excites you about the possibilities of a new opportunity, but keep in mind that in themselves, feelings are a poor decision-making tool. They're often wrong, and they almost always change.

Remember the coworker you found so annoying who later became a good friend? Or the time you were pumped up about a new job or business opportunity, only to be bored or frustrated by it six months later? And what about that manager who at first seemed cold and self-involved but eventually became a Mentor you could turn to for solid career advice?

(continued on page 13)

New courage and endurance

So picture it: <u>you</u> in charge of your thoughts.

<u>You</u> making the conscious choice to silence any negative self-talk that has the nerve to try to sneak in on your day.

<u>You</u> with new courage and endurance, no longer worn out by hopeless thinking.

And <u>you</u> taking hope-filled action that opens a channel of positive people and experiences that flows in both directions: out from you, but also back toward you...

You begin to attract people who think like you: colleagues, mentors, friends, and coworkers who share your hopeful outlook and approach to work and are working hard to create their own breakthroughs.

Since you value their balanced thinking and thoughtful opinions, they're your go-to people when you want to share a new idea or brainstorm a fresh solution. They're having lunch with someone you've been thinking you'd like to meet. They're making

a presentation at the networking event you're attending. They introduce you to influential people, let you know about exciting new opportunities, enjoy swapping good news with you, and clue you in to resources that will help you.

And you do the same for them. Your optimism uncovers fresh opportunities for your colleagues. Your reputation for designing creative solutions precedes you, putting you at the top of the list when challenging and high potential opportunities come up.

Because you insist on seeing the bright side, you make people feel healthy and hopeful. They seek out your company and freely share their ideas with you, confident that you'll find even the smallest grain of positive potential and help them expand on it.

Your faith in others increases their loyalty to you. Colleagues find you easy to be around and so likeable that they give you more of their time more readily. You're also more effective because it's much harder to say "No" to someone you like, no matter what the request.

Your credibility also gets a boost. If complaining is not your usual style, when you do choose to gripe or grumble

(continued from page 12)

Shop when you're feeling hungry, and you'll come home with every bag of junk food in aisles 9 and 10. Say what jumps into your mind when a coworker makes a mistake that costs you a day of work, and you'll hurt your relationship and maybe even your reputation. Avoid the tough conversation with a troubled employee because you're dreading it, and the situation is likely to get worse.

Feelings are flawed, fickle, and fleeting and in themselves, will often steer you wrong. It's just not possible to make good decisions when your mind is operating on information supplied only by your emotions. Factor them in, but focus on the bigger picture, set high expectations, and use your goals as the ultimate compass to steer you right.

in order to make a point, you're taken seriously rather than dismissed as someone who's always moaning.

Look at this ripple effect! Your involvement with positive people yields the very hope-filled, high potential experiences you're after.

Now who's the success magnet?

Let's move on to some practical suggestions for generating **Positive Power** in your work life…

Get tough (minded)

In *The Power of Optimism*, author Alan Loy McGinnis whose books have sold millions of copies, uses the phrase "tough-minded optimist" to talk about the mental and emotional strength that optimism requires. That's just spot on. "Tough mindedness" is a great way to describe the grit and mental stamina it takes to resist feelings and choose to see a bad situation through a positive, high expectation lens.

Then there's this encouragement from Teddy Roosevelt, 26th President of the United States: "The credit belongs to the man who is actually in the arena whose face is marred by dust and sweat and blood, who strives valiantly; who errs and comes short again and again…who at the best knows in the end the triumph of high achievement and who at the worst, if he fails, at least he fails while daring greatly."

Roosevelt was talking about persistence, no question. But between the lines there's something more: he was also hinting that history will not remember the people who just throw themselves into the arena again and again, unprepared and vulnerable because they haven't learned anything from past mistakes, but rather those who learn from the dust and sweat and grow from their experiences, changing their approach for the next time…and the next. In the world of work, persistence is essential, but by itself, it's not enough for success. It won't help you to just keep showing up, without growing in knowledge and skill. Ditto optimism. It's great to have high expectations, but success isn't going to chase you simply because you expect it to.

To dare *greatly* is to expect the best and to persist, but also to *evolve*. That's being tough minded: learning from past experiences (Which strategies worked best? What do past successes tell you about your strengths? What resources and people helped most? Who can open new doors for you next time?), standing up again, dusting yourself off if need be, and heading back into the arena (meeting, sales month, tough conversation) newly prepared, fresh and ready.

We'd like to linger on the topic of daring greatly, a habit essential for any breakthrough and a source of passion for us personally. We've seen too many talented people with so much to offer get tripped up by their expectation of a smooth and easy path to success.

> **They're easily discouraged by obstacles,** unwilling to push past even the first or second disappointment they experience in their quest to reach a goal. Instead, they accept setbacks as some type of cosmic signal that they should stop, no matter how important the dream or breakthrough is to them. This easy frustration leads them to give up on a quest long before they've given it all they've got.

They may believe persistence alone is enough, that if they show up every day and keep plugging away, eventually the dream will be within reach. But it's been a long time since the business world rewarded us for simply showing up and doing our jobs. Whether you're self-employed or work for a company, the bar on what's considered excellent performance keeps rising. Competition for every position, project, and contract intensifies every year, and all our jobs demand much more than just persistence. Mere dependability and truly breakthrough performance are miles apart.

They miss the partial solution. After a grueling year looking for a new job, John finally gets an offer that would put him in a higher league with greater long-term potential. But as he stares at the disappointing salary letter, he thinks, "I can't accept that job for less than a 20 percent raise! It doesn't matter how great the long-term potential is. I'm not taking less that I deserve! I'll wait until something better comes along." It's not the perfect solution, but it offers potential that sure beats staying put.

They don't recognize interim successes. Consider the too-proud salesperson who misses an opportunity to build a highly leveragable relationship with a global company because the initial order is modest: "I don't care that this order will get me in the door at this company. It's too small for me to waste my time on it."

They're too sensitive. "I worked on that report for a month, and when I presented it, they said it had some merit—just *some*. I felt like they gave me a C+. That's the last time I make a suggestion to that group."

They generalize a setback, using disempowering self-talk that makes the setback sound (and feel) like a permanent condition:

- "This *always* happens when I try something new."
- "I'm just *never* going to work well on a team."
- "I *never* get my facts straight."
- "I'm *constantly* messing up."
- "I *am just not* a leader."

Listen for the language of self defeat: "always," "never," "constantly," and "I am just not."

They use "Why me?" self-talk: "Why me? I've always worked so hard/gone the extra mile/been friendly and accommodating! And why did this have to happen now? I just bought/sold the house, started/left the job, bought/sold the business, had the baby, took the loan…?"

If you start reacting to a setback in any of these ways, stop. The moment you hear yourself say, "I blew it again," "I don't understand why this happens to me all the time," "I can't" or "That's it! I'm done trying," zip it! Stop talking, and get your feet moving—anywhere. Go out for a head-clearing walk or drive, get involved in an activity, call your Mom. Do whatever you can to break this train of thought because it will only take you down, down, down. Nothing positive will come of it.

So you didn't get the assignment, promotion, raise, or the credit you deserve. Take time for some healthy venting (see page 46). Then, get constructive—fast—by asking yourself what we call **The Good Questions**, five simple prompts we

Leader Point

For decades, running the mile in under four minutes was considered impossible, beyond the physical capacity of the human body. But in 1954, Roger Bannister, a 25-year-old British medical student, proved this belief wrong by running a mile in 3 minutes and 59.4 seconds on the Iffley Road track in Oxford, England in front of 3,000 spectators.

More amazing than the achievement itself was the aftermath. Though for years, runners had tried without success to break the four minute mile, within six weeks of Bannister's achievement, the record was broken again. Within a few years, the mile had been run in less than four minutes hundreds of times.

The runners had not broken through a physical barrier, but a mental one, a belief as concrete and insurmountable an obstacle as a solid brick wall.

What's your team's four-minute mile? And what about you as a leader? What belief has created the illusion of a physical barrier that's holding you back? What steps can you take to begin deconstructing these obstacles for your team and for yourself?

created to give you positive, future-focused and action-based answers:

1. "What did I do right (there's always something!)?"

2. "What did I learn? How can I apply this in the future?"

3. "What would have been the best possible outcome in a situation like this?"

4. "How can I work to bring that about next time?"

5. "What small step can I take right now to begin setting this in motion?"

For a free, printable version of The Good Questions you can post in your workspace, go to *www.breakthroughskills.com.*

Use your answers to channel your energy into constructive action:

- A phone call to build a bridge that reconnects you with someone you've argued with.

- The healthy audacity to explore a brand new sales territory no one on the team has even thought of.

Working Wisdom

Hold tight to your "impossible" dreams

"Start your own business?...

"Close that huge sale?...

"Run the Marketing Department? ...

"Earn a PhD?...

...do you know how hard that is?"

Sometimes it seems as if all you need to do is mention an exciting, ambitious goal, and suddenly the naysayers come out of the woodwork. Many of them have good intentions. They're trying to save you from the disappointment and frustration of what they believe is a sure failure. They may even have personal experience with the quest you're embarking on. Having tried it and failed, they want to help you avoid the pain and heartache they experienced.

But ask anyone who's achieved the "impossible," and you'll find that a positive outlook and self-belief were as critical to their victory as any action they took. These assets gave them the unshakable confidence they needed to reach the goal.

(continued on page 20)

(continued from page 19)

Psychologist and author Piero Ferrucci once wrote, "How often—even before we began—did we declare a task 'impossible'? And how often have we construed a picture of ourselves as being inadequate? A great deal depends on the thought patterns we choose and on the persistence with which we affirm them."

Believe in your impossible dream and be determined to do whatever it takes to reach it. Surround yourself with Trusted Colleagues and Mentors, and refuse to let any naysayer discourage you. Gird yourself with some powerful internal responses. When you hear...

• "No one's ever done it before," think: So, I'll be the first. I'm a trailblazer!

• "People have tried that and failed," think: But I haven't tried it yet, and I won't fail because I will make it work.

• "It can't be done," think: All I needed for inspiration was <u>one</u> example of someone who succeeded at achieving this dream to know that it can be done. And I've got that.

Don't waste your precious energy defending your dreams to the naysayers. Spend it instead on hope-filled action to create the work you love.

- A job search down new, exciting avenues you never would have explored if you weren't holding that pink slip in your hand.

- Your hand raised to volunteer for a project when the last one you ran, which was roundly criticized as a waste of money, taught you how to manage expenses better.

- Admitting that your company is on the brink because you started to ignore your loyal customers... and gathering the courage to ask these customers back.

- Going back to the boss who shut you down three times with a fourth idea that reflects her feedback on the previous three.

- Acting with confidence that a key employee's resignation will enable you to find someone even more qualified to fill her position.

Turn to your Success Partners for help. Take a Trusted Colleague or Mentor aside and explain that you're working to break a habit of defeated thinking in the face of obstacles, and you'd like some help. A coaching client who ran what had been a thriving retail business once confided that she was, in her words, "desperate to remember the good things about managing a team of people." Years of disappointments and frustrations with employees had taken their toll, and she knew her attitude about her current employees, like the way she immediately assumed they were being less than honest about their reasons for calling in sick or coming in late to work, were demotivating everyone and hurting her business.

Who are your Success Partners and how can they help you break through to new heights? Find out in *The THINK! Workbook*. Visit *www.breakthroughskills.com* to get your copy.

Your issue may be smaller: you may take "no" for an answer and back down too easily. Maybe you need to operate with more confidence, even when you don't feel confident. Perhaps you exaggerate the impact of every small mistake you make. It could be that good partial solutions are often staring you in the face, but you don't recognize them.

Regardless of how defeated thinking is holding you back, it's time to turn a page. Confide in a Success Partner. Get help... and get tough.

Watch your media diet

For his film *Super Size Me*, Morgan Spurlock, a 33-year-old documentary filmmaker who began his project in good health, wanted to trace the effects of eating a steady diet of junk food. For a month, Spurlock decided his three squares would consist of nothing but burgers, shakes, and lots of fries. To give the film credibility and get a scientific read on the health effects of eating this food for 30 days, Spurlock hired three doctors to monitor his health throughout the project.

In the end, his physicians documented effects that could only be called shocking—even to them—including dangerously elevated cholesterol, nausea, stomach and chest pains, liver damage, and depression. Spurlock took the time to document something we know intuitively: junk food is bad for you, and now we know, *really* bad.

None of us would ever consciously do this to ourselves, however tempting fast food might be. But food comes in other forms. For instance, we're on a media diet too, and steady meals of negative news and uninspiring entertainment affects what's in our minds…and what's on our minds. While there's plenty of good media to consume—balanced news reports, thought-provoking articles, great music, inspiring books, and good movies—too much of the business news seems to say that all executives are greedy, every business practice favors employers at employees' expense, and scandal is everywhere. Even good news is never really *good*. Sure, the story of a pharmaceutical company providing free medication to AIDS patients in Zambia *sounds* positive, but if you read the article carefully, it seems like there's more to the story, some self-serving intention lurking beneath the surface.

Sure, a new top executive's intention to reinvigorate a failing business by changing the product line and acquiring another company *sounds* noble, but the subtext of the story is that he'll probably have to fire people in the process, and you *know* he's going to make millions at the same time.

Even good economic news is negated by predictions of the next Big Crash: "The market closed up 300 points today in response to news of higher-than-expected first quarter earnings. Economists fear a major recession is unavoidable."

After consuming all this, who has the emotional stamina—or any tangible reason for that matter—to feel hopeful and optimistic?

In a now famous example of how the entertainment media influences us, when the movie *ET* was in development in the early 1980s, producer Steven Spielberg approached the Mars Corporation with the idea of making M&Ms the alien ET's candy of choice in the movie. Mars made the colossal mistake of declining the offer.

When Spielberg later approached Hershey's with the same idea, they accepted, and Reese's Pieces became ET's favorite candy. The technique is called product placement: the use of packaged products in visual media such as movies and TV shows as a way to increase sales of these products, and ad agencies consider it a highly effective element of a brand's sales and marketing strategy. How effective? When *ET* hit theaters in 1982, sales of Reese's Pieces, which had been floundering until that point, jumped 80 percent.

If you've ever had to change your diet, you probably know that a good way to start is to build your awareness of what you're eating by keeping a food diary, a record of everything that passes your lips in a week.

It works here too: take an honest look at your media diet by making a list of the media you read, watch, and listen to in a given week, and rating its level of positive inspiration on a scale from 1 to 5, with 1 being "positive and uplifting" and 5 being "negative and uninspiring." At the end of the week, review your list to see what's been on your media diet. What do you notice? Is the majority of the media you're consuming positive, balanced, informative and helpful? Or a mindless, negative waste of time?

What's on my media diet?

Media I "consumed" this week	Positive Inspiration Level Scale 1–5 [1=negative and uninspiring; 5=positive and uplifting]
News	
Magazines	
Music	
Books	
TV Shows	
Movies	
TOTAL	

The higher your total score, the better.

If it turns out you might benefit from making some changes, become more selective: start to shift the balance toward positive and uplifting content and away from negative, unbalanced, or pessimistic messages.

People count, too. Who's in your circle? Are they positive, passionate, driven, and upbeat, or drainers who pull you down and leave you feeling dull and empty, maybe even angry? Check yourself: after spending time with a certain friend or coworker, do you feel encouraged or demotivated? Hopeful or cynical? Confident or insecure? When you share good news with them or talk about an idea that excites you, are you buoyed by their enthusiasm or discouraged by their skepticism?

A longtime friend and colleague of ours who built a multi-million dollar insurance brokerage before retiring a decade ago once confided that in the years he spent working part-time after school in the factories on Manhattan's Lower East side in the 1940s, he discovered an important secret of success. "I noticed there were two groups of people," he told us. "One group sat around and bellyached all day about anything and everything: the boss, the work, the company, the world. The second group never complained. They kept busy all the time, and they were the ones who got all the best jobs and the 'atta boys.' I was just a kid, but I could tell that I should keep my distance from the first group or I'd get pulled in. That scared me more than anything because somehow I knew it meant I might never leave the Lower East side. I was determined to make it out. And I did."

Working Wisdom

Beware the deficit finders

Imagine you've worked hard to finish a report for one of your clients, and today, you're meeting with the client team. The only item on the agenda: your report.

You're confident the report is solid and excited about the chance to discuss it with the team. Your notepad is open to a fresh sheet of paper, and your pen is poised.

"Okay, I'll go first," someone says. "Here's what I don't like about it," followed by a litany of complaints and criticisms of your work.

Then, it's someone else's turn. She begins with, "Well, in addition to what he doesn't like, here's what I don't like," and then adds to the list of criticisms.

Slowly, painfully, they make their way around the table, each taking a turn finding deficits in your report. You're more distressed and embarrassed by the minute.

Finally, it's over.

"Thanks," you say numbly. "I'll get right on those changes."

(continued on page 27)

Take yourself to lunch

Let's turn the tables for a minute: what's it like to be around _you_? For example, after eating lunch with you, do your coworkers feel hopeful and positive? And what about everyday conversations? After talking to you, do friends feel encouraged and energized? Or something else?

Standing in your own shoes behind your own eyes, it can be tough to know the affect you have on people or the buzz that lingers in a room after you leave it. So tough, that some of the most talented and valuable people have no idea how negative their every-day conversations can sound. People are sometimes shocked to discover that even something as simple as their answer to the question, "How are you?" says a lot about them, sending a clear message about their outlook and level of optimism. How do you answer?

"Hangin in."

"Same old same old."

"All right, I guess."

"Could be better, could be worse."

Or the all-too-common brush off: "Swamped" (in other words, "Stay away from me, if you don't mind.")

Or maybe your answer is "Fine" or "Great," but your tone, facial expression, or body language says otherwise.

Other unconscious ways to send a negative message: sarcastic remarks about the team, the company, or your customers ("Oh joy! We tried that last year, only then it was called the XYZ initiative" or "He wants us to give him a weekly list of his orders. Like I need that much extra work from one customer right now"), a roll of the eyes in reaction to someone's enthusiasm, a sigh when the phone rings, a kneejerk "No" or "The problem with that is..." in response to every new idea.

If you're squirming a bit because all this sounds familiar, give yourself some slack. Maybe you picked up on a negative vibe at work and began to talk this way without realizing it. Or maybe you made a conscious decision to laugh at sarcastic remarks and cynical jokes so you'd be included in the group. It's understandable: act like Mr. or Ms. Sunshine in front of a bunch of cynics, and at best you'll

(continued from page 26)

You've just been the victim of a team of deficit finders. Be careful not to assume they mean harm; many of us were trained to think that finding mistakes and problems is the sign of a job well done. But this approach can backfire, as in this example where you leave the meeting knowing plenty about what they didn't like and don't want and nothing about what they did like and do want.

Ironically, the team may actually like what you've done overall, but their style of providing feedback doesn't communicate this. You have the input you need to get rid of what they don't like, but not to amplify what they do like.

There is an alternative, though, and it's within your power to bring it about. It's asset-based feedback, or you might call it constructive feedback: helpful comments and reactions that you can build on. You can set yourself up to receive this type of feedback simply by asking asset-based questions at the start of the meeting or conversation. Here are some examples based on this scenario:

"From experience, I know the best way to decide next steps is

(continued on page 28)

(continued from page 27)

for us to talk about what you liked in the report and what you'd like to see more of. Would you please tell me:

- *Overall, what elements of my approach were most effective?*

- *Would you identify for me the two or three ideas you liked most and why?*

- *What was the most important or valuable finding?*

- *What additional information would you like to see in the next draft?*

- *How can I expand on what I've done to give it more impact?"*

In addition to setting an upbeat tone for the meeting, we bet your deficit finders will be relieved that you've taken charge and helped them help you. Plus, they'll leave the meeting feeling more positive, though they may not know exactly why.

For more on the topic of constructive feedback, you may also want to see Part 2 of our book Hot Situations, Cool Heads: How to Thrive When Conflict Arrives. *You can get a copy at www. breakthroughskills.com.*

be teased and embarrassed; at worst, you'll be dismissed as someone who just doesn't "get it" and left out of the loop completely.

Some people make the mistake of thinking skepticism and the sarcasm that often go along with it are the mark of sophistication, the sign of a deep, analytical mind. Nothing's going to fool them. They don't accept things at face value and instead keep digging until they find the catch or the "real story." At work, they're the deficit finders, the people who uncover the defects in every project, the glitches in every program, and the flaw in every idea. "It'll never work," "Here's what I don't like about that idea," and "Sure, *that'll* happen" are some of their favorite phrases. They don't rest until everyone is discouraged, demotivated, or embarrassed at how ridiculous their idea looks after it's been julienned.

In his book *The Optimistic Child* (HarperPerennial, 1996), Martin Seligman, former President of the American Psychological Association, wrote about cynicism this way:

Step Out of the Box with a Bang! • A Rapid-Read Handbook™

"I have studied pessimism for the last 20 years and in more than one thousand studies involving more than half a million children and adults, pessimistic people do worse than optimistic people in three ways. First, they get depressed much more often. Second, they achieve less at school, on the job, and on the playing field than their talents augur. Third, their physical health is worse than optimists. So holding a pessimistic view of the world may be the mark of sophistication, but it is a costly one."

Regardless of how or why it begins, left unchecked (and maybe even unnoticed), this type of thinking is a boa constrictor that quickly winds its way around your professional life and starts to squeeze tight and make sure you're not going anywhere. No matter how strong you are, skepticism and cynicism start to affect what you believe about yourself and your future…

…every idea sounds unworkable.

   …every opportunity looks too good to be true.

      …and worst of all, no one seems completely trustworthy.

So you don't even bother to apply for that new position or to pursue that big client or ambitious project because it probably won't work out anyway. Why waste your time?

You don't make the effort to introduce yourself to an influential person because they probably won't actually help you. Why bother putting yourself out there?

You don't volunteer to take on extra responsibility or new experiences because they won't lead to anything. Why just make more work for yourself?

Working Wisdom

Feet on the ground

Is it possible to go too far in your efforts to have a positive, energizing influence on the people you work with and for?

You bet it is.

A client of ours waited years for a promotion that never came before she realized that wishing everyone a "Happy First Day of Spring," gushing over the promise of every idea, and using the word "wonderful" all the time were hurting her credibility. She was considered too lighthearted and easygoing to be a serious player with leadership in her future.

Remember, a certain amount of feet-on-the-ground realism is a must for building a reputation as a sincere, credible, and balanced professional who's truly breakthrough-bound.

Before long, the people who influence your success believe you don't have serious aspirations for the future; you've topped out where you are and aren't interested in going any further. They stop recommending you for new positions, referring you to high potential prospects, and involving you in exciting projects.

Talk about self defeating!

But some good news: negative talk is just a habit, and breaking it isn't difficult. In fact, the toughest part is simply becoming aware of how often you say things like:

- "The problem with that is…"

- "I'll believe *that* when I see it."

- "Yeah, right."

- "Just maybe."

- "I think not."

- "Give me a break!"

Erase these kinds of phrases from your mind. Then on purpose—that is, whether you feel like it or not—radiate more optimism:

- When someone asks you how you are, answer "Good" or "Great" in a tone that says you mean it.

- Speak in positive terms about the company, its leadership, and colleagues who are not in the room. If you can't, don't say anything.

- When something does go wrong, cut the people involved some slack and encourage everyone to move on.

- Don't generate, listen to, or repeat rumors or gossip of any kind.

- Say "Thanks" more often.

- Make eye contact and smile more often.

- Encourage people to reach for their goals. Show interest and get excited for them by asking them questions about their plans. And never (ever) crush someone's hopes or criticize their dreams.

- Listen only to real problems and legitimate complaints and respond empathetically with, "That must be tough" or "That sounds like a lot to handle." Then, share a few constructive ideas or brainstorm solutions together.

- Practice phrases like: "I/we sure can," "Let me/us be responsible," "My/our pleasure," "Sure thing," "You bet," "Absolutely," and "That sounds interesting. Tell me more."

- Nix: "Swamped," "Hangin' in," "The problem with that is," "I don't know what to tell you," and "Can't be done."

Out of the question: brand new potential

Fresh out of college, Dan was hired as an intern at an insurance company, a fast-track program of six-month rotations around the business for three years. By the end of his first year, he was doing pretty well. He'd finished a few highly visible projects and was earning a reputation for being smart and aggressive. There was just one problem: Dan was also earning a reputation for having a fit whenever he didn't get his way.

The day he was called into the Vice President's office, Dan tried to look casual. He walked in and sat on the sumptuous leather couch in the man's enormous office.

"Dan, you're fired," said the VP right off the bat.

"I am?"

"Yes. Pack up your desk, and Security will escort you out. They're waiting outside my office for you. Thanks and good luck."

Dan managed to stand up on shaky legs and start to walk out.

"Wait a minute," the VP said. "Come back."

Dan turned. "Yes?"

"You're not fired, Dan. I was trying to make a point. I could fire you right now, like I just did. And you know what? *It would not be fair.* But I could still do it, and you'd still have to figure out what to do next. If you want to be successful, you have to get over this idea you seem to have that every-thing has to be fair and make sense to you. Things are not always going to go your way, and the sooner you figure that out, not only will you succeed, you'll be a lot happier."

Dan, who today is a General Manager at a global construction company, left that office a changed person. "Afterward," he says,

"I figured out how to ask myself just one question when something went wrong: 'What can I do next that will turn things around?' It was definitely a turning point, and I owe a lot to that VP."

When the meeting doesn't go as planned, when the plum opportunity is handed to someone else, when the long-awaited promotion doesn't come, when the project gets derailed, sales slump or the phone stops ringing, our sense of fair play takes a hit. It's like the kid inside yells, "Hey, no fair! Not after...

- ...all the work I did."

- ...how long I've waited."

- ...how loyal I've been."

- ...I've been such a team player."

- ...I helped out every chance I got."

- ...I took the time to finish my degree and she didn't."

We want to know _why_. We immediately begin to ask the most uninspiring questions possible—questions that rehash and analyze the problem: "Why did this happen? Who's responsible? Why did they do that? Isn't this the third time this year?" Because these questions zero in on what's missing,

Working Wisdom

The David is in the marble

Michelangelo once characterized his genius with great humility by saying that his masterpieces were already in the marble and that his job was just to take away the extra stone so they could be seen.

Could it be that there's a David or a Pietà in every situation, and that any of us, just by asking better questions, can get rid of the stuff in the way and allow it to emerge?

The question would probably spark an interesting debate. But the real issue isn't whether the David is in marble or not. The real issue is that if you begin to believe that by asking better questions—questions that unleash the positive potential in any situation— you have the power to let a masterpiece emerge, you may be right.

And just imagine the possibilities if you are.

what's wrong, and who's at fault, we call them deficit-based questions.

Deficit-based questions have a negative supposition built into them. When you realize you overlooked an important detail, for example, a question like, "Why do I always miss critical details?" instructs your brain to be on the lookout for an answer that begins: "I always miss critical details because..." The question focuses your thinking on what's wrong and who's to blame (in this case, you).

But it also does something more serious: it supposes that you *always* miss critical details. Without realizing it, through the simple act of asking this question, you've limited yourself. You've said, in effect, that you're the type of person who always misses critical details, which means you expect yourself to do it again and again.

A question like, "What part of the process is broken?" assumes that the process is broken (it may or may not in fact *be* broken). Your brain is now on the lookout for when and where and who: "The problem started in Stage 2 of the process when Jack's team..."

A few more examples:

> **Deficit-based:** "When will John realize just how demotivating his attitude is?"
> **Negative Supposition:** John's entire attitude is pulling the team down.
> **Answer:** "John will realize how demotivating his attitude is when..."

Deficit-based: "Why is morale so low around here?"

Negative Supposition: Low morale is a serious problem for this team.

Answer: "Morale is low because…"

Deficit-based: "Why are customer complaints rising in our Atlanta store?"

Negative Supposition: The Atlanta store is doing something very wrong.

Answer: "Complaints are rising in Atlanta because…"

Deficit-based questions serve a single, uninspiring, energy-zapping purpose: to look backward and study the problem. Closely, for a long time, and with a magnifying glass if one is handy. Answers to deficit-based questions describe and analyze the problem. And—this is important—at some point, they will name names. In other words, they will identify who is responsible for the problem so that person can be called on the carpet, humbly accept the blame, and fix things, ASAP.

What type of mood does this create on a team? What beliefs and views does it foster?

- "I better be careful that problems aren't traced back to me. Better send lots of memos to cover myself and copy everyone I can think of."

- "Better not take the risk of trying something new. If it doesn't go well, I'll face the blame."

- "I need to be careful who I trust."

- "The people who get rewarded around here are those who find and fix problems, not those who come up with new ideas."

As Frank Barrett, a professor at the Naval Postgraduate School, wrote in his article "Creating Appreciative Learning Cultures," "Operating from a problem-solving mentality risks reaffirming the status quo." In a problem-solving culture, "people often develop defensive postures...they become more concerned with escaping blame than with discovering new approaches. This causes greater separation between people, making it difficult to build trust. Defensive posturing does not encourage experimentation or creative thinking."

But we can take the very same kinds of questions, and give them an asset-based makeover, like so:

"What went wrong?" **[Deficit-based]**

can become...

"What went right, and how can I use that to rise above this situation?" or "I'm determined to make something good happen here. What do I have working in my favor?" **[Asset-based]**

Asset-based questions zoom your mental lens in on the positive potential in any situation, but they're especially valuable after a setback because they concentrate your mind and energy on possibilities instead of problems, and on the future instead of the past. Through asset-based questions, you're no longer studying the nature of the problem in detail: when it started, who's responsible, or where the process is broken. Instead, you're focused on how you can use what you've learned to create a more positive future.

Here's the first sample question again:

"Why do I always miss the critical details?"

and the answer your brain is seeking:

"I always miss critical details because…"

Now, here's the same question after it gets an asset-based makeover:

"How can I be certain to catch all the critical details in my work in the future?"

and the answer your brain is now seeking:

"Here's what I can do to be certain I catch all the critical details in my work in the future…"

When you answer *this* question—which has the built-in positive supposition that it's possible for you to be more thorough in the future—you no longer waste time rehashing your mistake, but instead plan the steps you'll take next time: the additional research you'll do, the people who can help you with fact-checking, the amount of extra time you'll allow for a project to be certain you're not rushed when you need to double-check essential information, etc.

What a difference! Same issue. Different approach: from deficit-based to asset-based. Totally different outcome: from hopeless to hopeful. From current problem to future potential. Now, you're breakthrough-bound.

Let's makeover the other sample questions:

> **Deficit-based:** "Where did the problem start? What part of this process is broken?"
> **Asset-based makeover:** "Where did the process have the greatest momentum?" or "What steps can we take to produce the best possible finished product next time?"
> **Positive supposition:** Part of the process worked well or producing a great finished product is possible next time.

Deficit-based: "When will John realize just how demotivating his attitude is?"

Asset-based makeover: "What strengths does John bring to the project? How can we bring those out and leverage them fully?"

Positive supposition: John has unique strengths that can be helpful to the project.

Deficit-based: "Why is morale so low around here?"

Asset-based makeover: "When have we had high morale in the past, and how can we recreate those conditions?"

Positive supposition: This team knows how to work well together. We've done that before, and we can do it again.

Deficit-based: "Why are customer complaints rising in our Atlanta store?"

Asset-based makeover: "How can we provide our Atlanta customers with the best/most memorable service experience? What service qualities will let us eclipse the competition in Atlanta?"

Positive supposition: We have what it takes to give our customers the best total service experience in the area.

Notice certain qualities asset-based questions share. Typically, they:

- Are stated in the affirmative ("What would be the *ideal outcome* in this situation?" "What's been *your best experience* with…?").

- Encourage storytelling ("_Tell me about_ the time you..." "_How did_ all that come about?")

- Illuminate new possibilities ("_What would happen if_ we were able to successfully...?")

- Are open-ended, encouraging dialogue and freedom to think and consider "what ifs?" and other possibilities ("_What if_ you were at the helm? _What steps would you take_ to get everyone jazzed about the program?")

Here are some asset-based questions and sentence stems to keep at the ready:

For a free, printable version of The Great Questions, a unique list of asset-based questions you can post in your workspace, go to _www.breakthroughskills.com._

1. "What do you expect will happen when you successfully..."

2. "What did you enjoy most about..."

3. "Tell me about what went right in that situation..."

4. "Think of a time a similar situation went well. Tell me about it."

5. "What do you think was really making the process work at such a high level?"

6. "What was the climate in the business at that point that enabled you to take that successful step/action?"

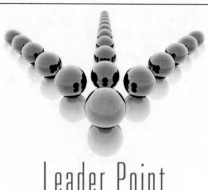

Leader Point

When you begin to challenge your team by asking them asset-based questions, you'll see an immediate, dramatic change in how they think and act, in particular how they respond to a setback. Asset-based questions, and more to the point, the energizing dialogue they spark, put a stop to negative, defeated thinking before it has a chance to begin.

In fact, whenever we introduce a team to asset-based thinking, we watch as members begin to sit up taller, their faces come alive and their voices get louder and more excited about what they're saying. The change is so significant that we often say it's like watching a room go from gray to Technicolor before our eyes.

A great time to introduce your team to asset-based questions is at the start of a project or goal. Challenge the team with questions like these:

1. "What three wishes do we have for making this effort a positive, powerful experience? What two steps can each of us take to create this positive energy and turn these wishes into reality?"

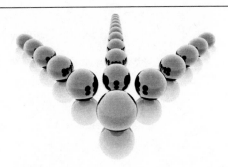

2. "What changes and trends are we seeing in the business world/our industry/our profession that excite us and give us confidence in the potential of this effort?"

3. "If we had no constraints, how would we approach this?"

4. "What single result would make us walk away from this effort declaring it a smashing success? What two things can we do right now to begin bringing this about?"

5. "What's been our best experience with a similar endeavor from the past that ended successfully? Let's talk about what went right. What elements or ideas can we apply to this effort?"

6. "What three words would we like to come to mind when people talk about our achievements a year or two from now? What two things can we do right now to begin bringing this about?"

7. "What would make everyone involved in this effort feel like an owner of the outcome? What two things can we do right now to begin bringing this about?"

8. "Who are our internal champions? What two steps can we take to excite them about our effort's progress/potential?"

Working Wisdom

Language that devours

"Stop doing that. Your face is going to get stuck that way!" Remember Mom's warning? Maybe she was right. Repeated behaviors—especially behaviors you stop examining or questioning—are habit forming.

And while that can be a positive when the habit is healthy like punctuality or speaking up for what you believe in, it can also be a problem when the habit is unhealthy like defensiveness or talking about yourself in negative ways.

Whether you say them aloud or just repeat them in your mind, negative words about yourself harm your hope and self belief. Here are seven words we forbid our clients to use in reference to themselves:

- *Failure*
- *Loser*
- *Quitter*
- *Stupid*
- *Untalented*

(continued on page 43)

Language that empowers

Asset-based thinking goes beyond the questions you ask. It includes your general word choice too. Think about the difference between telling an employee, "Don't take a break before 10 am," and "Feel free to take a break after 10 am." The same message stated in positive (asset-based) terms is much easier to hear and act on. It's also more respectful and empowering to the listener which means it's more likely to be heard, understood, and acted upon.

Asset-based language is open-ended and future-focused, and it encourages dialogue. Take a look at these examples:

Before: Deficit-based	After: Asset-based
Neglected to	Need to
Lacks	Needs to include
Too difficult/beyond our capabilities	Will challenge/stretch our abilities/resources substantially
Struggle to	Strive to
Inaccessible	Need to be made accessible
Only 40 percent said	60 percent said
Problem	Chance/opportunity
Deviates from	Needs to better align with
Limited	Can be enhanced, leaves room for growth, shows improvement opportunity

Discontinue	Finalized/brought to a close so we can introduce next steps
Overlooks or excludes	Needs to more fully capture
Mistake	Something that needs to be added or enhanced; chance/opportunity
It won't be ready until after Tuesday.	It will be ready by Wednesday.
Don't forget…	Please remember…
You failed to sign the other copy.	Please sign the other copy too.
You never called me.	I'm so glad to hear from you!

(continued from page 42)

- *Disappointment*

- *Stuck*

We're also on the lookout for "can't," "always," "never," and other universal slap-ons that limit our clients' thinking and can pierce their potential like a sword.

And a hard truth: these words also absolve you of the responsibility to try again. Use a few of them repeatedly, and before long, you give in to hopelessness and give up on the quest. That can feel a whole lot easier than continuing to persist, especially after a big setback. It's a relief to declare defeat with an "I'm-such-a-loser" sigh rather than go back into the arena and fight. But the relief is temporary and quickly replaced by the frustration of staying right where you are, or worse, abandoning your dreams.

Make these (and any other negative words you've heard yourself use) your forbidden words too, not only in your breakthrough quest, but in your quest for a happy, healthy life.

Take a moment to think about how you'd feel on the receiving end of deficit-based language versus asset-based language. Notice how the phrases in the Deficit-based column tend to shut down conversation and cause defensive reactions. Accusatory words like "overlooks," "excludes," "neglected to" and "too difficult/beyond our capabilities" tend to put you on the defensive, as do statements like, "You failed to sign the other copy" and "You never call me." Hearing these words, you may feel guilty or as if you need to explain yourself to justify your actions.

On the other hand, the language in the Asset-based column is forward-facing, affirming, and hopeful (there's a "chance/opportunity," "It will be ready," "…can be enhanced"). This language also suggests positive action ("Please sign the other copy" and "Needs to more fully capture") and conveys your respect for the listener and high expectations for the situation.

Words can have creative or destructive power. You choose which power you'll tap.

Don't be fooled: asset-based language does look for the silver lining and sees the glass as half-full, but this is not sugarcoating, window-dressing, or spin. Asset-based language is a proven way to show your respect for others, empower them, and set the stage for easy collaboration and high achievement for yourself and your colleagues…and that's true whether you're an individual performer, corporate leader, or business owner.

"In the long run, what is likely to be more useful," said Thomas White, former President, GTE Telephone Operations, "Demoralizing a successful workforce by concentrating on their failures or helping them over their last few hurdles by building a bridge with their successes? Don't get me wrong, I'm not advocating mindless happy talk…We can't ignore problems, we just need to approach them from the other side."

To shift from deficit-based to asset-based language, tuck a few of these phrases in the back of your mind and use them as often as you can:

- "Why don't we try something new?"
- "We can make that even better."
- "Here's the upside…"
- "I see a hidden win here."
- "Let's think constructively about this for next time…"

- "Here's what we can do in the future…"

- "What if we tried…"

- "I think we're on the right track. Now, let's…"

- "That's right, and…"

- "We can do a lot with that idea."

- "Have you considered…"

- "You sparked my interest, tell me more."

Leader Point

One of the greatest ways leaders can use asset-based language is to recognize everyone's unique genius—the one-of-a-kind combination of experience and skill each person brings to the team.

Think of how productive and loyal your team will be when you routinely describe each person in terms of their unique genius and its irreplaceable value:

- "As our team's operations expert, John knows how to keep everyone's feet on the ground when we brainstorm solutions. He keeps us focused."

- "Michaela, our team's creative genius, sparks my group's thinking and gets everyone's juices flowing."

- "Jackson's our newest addition. His fresh perspective has given us countless insights into best practices and how other companies are responding to the trends in our industry."

And, as always, as the leader goes, so goes the team. When you begin to practice an asset-based approach to recognizing everyone's unique talents and contributions, you'll find team members thinking and talking this way about each other...and about you. The result: and upward spiral of respect, cohesiveness, and success.

Venting lifts the burden

- "I need to get this off my chest."
- "Something's weighing on me."
- "This issue has been on my mind."
- "I've been feeling this heaviness lately."
- "We've got to get this issue out of the way if we're ever going to make progress."

Interesting that we often describe frustrations and disappointments as concrete, physical burdens. It's as if we know intuitively that these are real barriers pinning us down or blocking the way forward. And while we're rewarded in business for competently handling everything that comes our way, there's a limit to the number of times we can do that without needing to vent to a sympathetic friend or coworker.

Like the figure of Sisyphus in Greek mythology who strains to push his rock up the hill only to have it roll back down on him, at some point shouldering a burden alone is just too much of a strain. Venting gives voice to what's going on in your head and heart. As you talk with complete abandon, unworried and unhurried to someone you trust, an escape valve opens to release negative, unproductive thoughts, let you see new possibilities, and start fresh. You may remember the Rolaids® TV ad from years ago: "How do you spell relief?" We spell it V-E-N-T.

A good friend of ours—and truly one of the most balanced people we know—will sometimes call and say, "Okay, I need to complain. For the next five minutes, I don't want to hear anything constructive. I need to get this off my chest, so I'm going to let it rip. Ready?"

Venting is so important that we encourage you to try it, even if you're the type of person who prefers to keep things to yourself.

The benefits of releasing the negative energy created by verbalizing fearful, frustrated, or angry thoughts swirling around inside your head are many. To name a few:

> You can actually laugh at some of the fear-filled thoughts that don't seem silly in your head but sound truly ridiculous coming out of your mouth.

> You can get confirmation of your feelings, encouragement, and constructive ideas from someone you trust.

> You let go of negative feelings that could eventually affect your health.

These and other benefits of venting are not possible through books, courses, or any other kind of resource. Sometimes, nothing beats just talking it out, one to one.

Working Wisdom

The right partner

To make venting healthy and effective for you, be sure to choose the right person to confide in.

Because they're familiar with your job, your skills and experiences, and the people you work with, most often your best choice for a venting partner is one of your Trusted Colleagues or Mentors.

Among them, choose someone who:

• *Has the time to listen fully to you and is not distracted by work pressures.*

• *Has no stake in the topic and can listen objectively.*

• *Commits to letting all vented information go "in one ear and out the other"...no bringing it up at a later point to remind you what you said in this high emotional state.*

(continued on page 49)

A few caveats, though: venting can become ineffective and even damaging to your outlook if it's an end in itself, that is, if it never leads to a solution or confident expectation of a goal. The purpose of venting isn't to build a library of stories and reasons to be angry or down ("And you know what else she did?" "Well let me tell you again about what happened last week." "This happens every time I volunteer an idea around here. I've been counting...did you know this is the fifth time I've been shot down?") To qualify as truly healthy, venting must have a short lifespan. Once the issue is off your chest, you're done rehashing. No more detail. No more examples.

It's time to get constructive.

Venting is most effective when it's done with a Trusted Colleague or Mentor, someone you can trust to listen fully, and then as quickly as possible steer you toward constructive

Find out more about developing strong relationships with your Trusted Colleagues, Mentors, and Key Influencers in *The THINK! Workbook*. Visit *www.breakthroughskills.com* to get your copy.

solutions and hope-filled action. Your Trusted Colleagues are professional friends, usually peers, you can easily talk to and brainstorm with. They are your plain-spoken sounding boards who won't put lots of window-dressing on their feedback and won't let you get by with excuses. Trusted Colleagues broaden your perspective with input and insights you're not capable of on your own.

(continued from page 48)

• *Encourages you to stay focused on the true issues, never the personalities or personal lives of the people involved (since this could cause the conversation to devolve into a gossip session).*

• *Doesn't interject suggestions or solutions until you've finished venting,*

but...

• *Won't let you vent forever, and knows how and when to help you begin brainstorming constructive solutions.*

And be sure to flip these traits around and apply them to yourself when you're in the listener's role.

Examples:

- People you currently work with or worked with in the past

- Fellow members of professional or business organizations

- Business friends you've come to know through some aspect of your work (met through a vendor, attended a seminar together, etc.)

Your Mentors are people whose success you admire and would like to emulate. Mentors are role models whose support and advice prevent you from having to "reinvent the wheel" and save you from making the mistakes they made. Note that Mentors are usually a level or two above you in rank or achievement; they've earned a measure of success beyond yours.

Examples:

- A leader in your company

- A fellow business owner

- A boss or former boss
- A successful person in your profession or industry whom you know through a mutual colleague or membership in a professional organization

How's your gratitude attitude?

Have you ever been around someone who's impossible to impress? Someone who has seen it all, done it all, and has the T-shirts to prove it? Gratitude is a foreign idea to them. Whether it's a terrific business seminar, a delicious and fun lunch with coworkers, a successful meeting, or a slam dunk sale, they seem to accept it all as a matter of course. Successes and great times are either a given or maybe never quite good enough for them.

Take a moment to picture someone you know who thinks this way and ask yourself: are they happy? Positive? Excited about the future? Bright, open, receptive, energized?

In a word, optimistic?

Chances are, no.

That's because optimism and gratitude are closely tied. Once again, what we focus on is what we see, and what we see is a result set in motion. Focus on what you're grateful for at work, and you'll see more to be grateful for. You'll also be inspired and energized to create more of the same for yourself. Do it right, and do it regularly, and gratitude will lift your whole outlook.

Grateful thoughts also calm the grasping and striving that tend to fill our work days. They make us more content by turning what we have into enough, without adding a thing. They give us perspective by raising our awareness of the abundance of friendship, support, opportunity, and healthy challenge in our work lives. Like the Mentor whose advice smoothed out a tough business situation. A job with good medical coverage. Paid vacations and personal days. Free training programs. Business friendships that make work fun.

Use the following to spark positive thoughts that boost your gratitude attitude:

1. Three everyday things I'm grateful for:

2. Three significant achievements I'm grateful for:

Working Wisdom

Gorillas in our midst

We recently came across this inspiring vignette:

At a business seminar, attendees are shown a video clip of two people playing catch and told to count the number of times the ball goes back and forth between them. In the middle of the tape, a huge gorilla comes on the screen and waves at the camera. When the clip ends, people are asked what they thought of the gorilla. Every single person insists there was no gorilla, and when they're allowed to look at the clip again, they insist they're looking at a different video.

Once again, what we focus on is what we see...to the exclusion of all else, even, apparently, a hairy gorilla.

Start today to harness this incredible power by deciding what you will—and won't—concentrate on.

Working Wisdom

Job joy

"What's the secret of your success?" It seemed like a good question to ask the multi-million dollar salesperson we were profiling for an insurance magazine.

"I let people know how much I enjoy my job," he said. *"I actually say—even to the most senior business leader— 'I love my job, and I'm not going anywhere. I'll be here if you want to continue our conversation.' It sounds corny, but I'm absolutely sincere when I say this. My clients know I enjoy what I do, so they trust that I'll do it right. And, more to the point, people are naturally attracted to honesty and commitment. They want to be around it, so they want to be around me."*

What a delight it was to interview this man, a leader in his company and in his community where he co-sponsors a number of youth programs and sits on the boards of several community beautification projects.

(continued on page 53)

3. I'm grateful for _____

_____

_____, my greatest skill/strength, and _____

_____

and _____

_____ the people who helped me build this skill/strength.

4. I'm grateful for

_____,

my most Trusted Colleague, because:

5. I'm grateful for

_____,

my most important client, because:

6. I'm grateful for

_____, my

Mentor, because:

(continued from page 52)

The interview was filled with vitality and inspiration...all around a central theme of energizing his success by nurturing a deeply positive outlook about his work and his potential to contribute. At number 24 out of the 8,500 sales reps in his company, clearly he's doing something very right.

7. I'm grateful for _____

_____, a

Key Influencer of my success,

because:

"I enjoy the process as well as the success I generate in my work," he said. "I take more pleasure in building the relationships that lead to the sales than I do in the sales themselves."

Maybe the secret of success has been staring at us since we were kids: have fun and don't hesitate to let others know that you are. We reach higher heights when we simply take joy in the climb.

8. Yesterday, I overlooked the chance to be grateful for:

9. Today, I will thank:

10. Tomorrow, I will compliment:

Every day excellent

In 1996, business consultant Jim Collins and Stanford Professor Jerry Porras wrote an article for the *Harvard Business Review* in which they coined the term "Big Hairy Audacious Goals" or BHAGs. They needed a way to refer to a company's huge, long-term, pole vaults to success, 10 to 30 years in the making. Before long, the term had seeped into every business planning meeting and discussion about the future.

The phrase itself seems to be all but gone now. Still, it's a helpful tool for giving companies the expectation of relative permanence and the responsibility to make short-term choices that reflect their long-term intentions.

You may not have 10 to 30 year BHAGs (though power to you if you do!), but what about your career aspirations and pro-fessional passions? Do your short-term choices and everyday expectations support them? What do you expect will happen today? What choices will you make to ensure that you're right?

When we ask them these questions, too often our coaching clients stare at us blankly, unsure how to answer. They're not trick questions, just questions we don't really think about. "I don't know. Just the usual everyday stuff," comes the answer. Some people have faced the pain of disappointment so many times that as a defense mechanism, they set their expectations low and steel themselves for the worst:

- "I hope this meeting isn't a complete waste of time."

- "I hope the prospect doesn't send the contract back again asking for even more changes."

- "I hope I make it through this presentation without fainting."

How disempowering to hope only that a meeting isn't a waste of time! And why set the bar so low that your definition of a successful presentation is simply one during which you stay vertical? What about expecting to do well, enjoy giving the talk, and answer every question easily? And if these aren't enough of a stretch for you, lift the bar higher: expect to make your audience say "Aha!" at least twice and leave excited about taking the course of action you recommend. Then maybe pull out the stops and expect to get a standing ovation! Your expectations will determine the level you will rise to on the smaller, everyday challenges in your work life as well as on the larger, more significant ones.

Having positive expectations about the ordinary and routine in your work life gives you new energy for every task and builds your confidence in the process:

- "I'm expecting great things to come out of this meeting. We're going to resolve the most important issues and leave with clear action steps."

- "The prospect is going to be much more comfortable with the new terms I've included in the contract. I'm confident she'll sign this week."

- "I'm sure my business will thrive in its new location."

- "Jeff will introduce me to the right people at the conference."

- "I expect my conversation with the CEO to go well."

Notice that none of these has the high-fiving, "Way to go!" of an audacious or long-term goal achieved, but rather a steady, everyday level of positive expectation that energizes and empowers you to push forward toward your long-term goals and—this is important—love your work in the process. Not a bad payoff for simply kicking your expectations up a few notches.

Never stop thinking

Two people begin separate consulting practices. Each loses a critical contract. The first consultant takes her former client to lunch to find out why, gets good information about steps she can take to make her business more successful in the future, and actually ends up building a stronger bridge to the client who is impressed by her genuine concern about his company and interest in his ideas. The client eventually sends her future business, including referrals to his colleagues. The second consultant blames the loss on poor chemistry and lives with that supposition, never bothering to uncover the real reason.

Long term, who succeeds? Who founders?

Two people are scheduled to interview for a highly desirable position. One plans the interview, researching the position and the company, finding out about the principals of the firm and the markets in which it competes, and arrives at the interview early, feeling fresh, positive, and prepared for an enjoyable conversation. The other decides chances are slim he's going to get the job, so he may as well just "wing it." The questions will be the standard ones anyway. After all, job interviews are all the same.

Who gets called back and who doesn't?

Two people receive average ratings on their performance reviews. One accepts the feedback as valuable advice and uses it constructively to set new goals and improve his job performance. The other resents receiving the same feedback after working hard all year, views it as negative, is discouraged and demotivated, and shares his frustration with everyone who'll listen.

Who succeeds? Who stagnates?

It's so interesting that in each case, we can easily complete the story. We know what happens to the woman who believes she lost the client because of poor chemistry. She finds everything a struggle. Clients come and go, and while her business survives, it doesn't thrive, and there is little joy in her work. We can also guess what happens to the person who doesn't prepare for the job interview, and the employee who is demotivated by a poor performance review.

We also know what happens to their positive counterparts. The business owner moves effortlessly from client to client, relationships are built and doors open easily. She expands her business, which she finds fulfilling, and people enjoy working with and for her. The person who prepares for the job interview probably does get called back. The employee with the average review overlooks his embarrassment and discomfort,

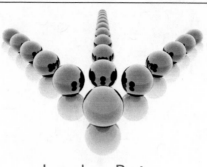

Leader Point

The people in your life are wearing signs—invisible at first glance, but crystal clear if you take the time to look—that say, "Notice me," "Compliment me," "Tell me I'm valuable," and "Please say thanks." And the people who act as if they don't need this kind of supportive feedback tend to be the ones who need it the most.

At work, no source of this feedback is more important than you. A simple compliment, well-timed and sincerely delivered, is without peer in its ability to encourage and motivate the people on your team. Sincere compliments also build great team loyalty.

So praise your team, and don't hold back. Be generous and specific with your compliments:

- "John here is a whiz at solving our IT issues."

- "Roberta is our ace when it comes to finding data."

- "We could not have gotten that filing in on time without Roger and Sue. They never let us lose sight of the timeline."

- "Liz, I appreciate the extra effort you gave last week to make this happen."

Make sure your compliments are:

- Based on specific achievements.
- Delivered one-on-one and publicly.
- Spread evenly across your full team.
- Based on a skill or achievement that truly matters to the person.

stands up, dusts himself off, and, armed with good information about his improvement opportunities, begins to press on to better experiences and rewards.

Look for a common theme in these stories, and for that matter, in the lives of all highly successful people: their minds are always working. In fact, they never stop thinking, asking future-focused questions that anticipate success and lead to positive action:

- "What if I took the client to lunch and asked why she fired me?"
- "How can I be over-prepared for this job interview?"
- "Now that I know what's expected of me, what steps can I take to make the most of this feedback to improve my performance in the coming year?"

Here are some sentence stems and questions to help you keep thinking:

- "Something I've seen work well in a similar situation that I'd like to try here is _____."
- "I need to get more information and insight in this situation. Who can I talk to?"

- "What resources (colleagues, books, classes...) are available to help me through this situation?"

- "What steps could I take right away to set a positive result in motion?"

Let it go

Forgiveness may not sound like a typical business topic, but it actually plays a huge role in using positive expectation to create breakthrough success. When you think you've been treated unfairly—someone didn't deliver on a key project element, backed out of a commitment, or unfairly criticized your work—forgiving the person frees up your time and your thought calories to once again see positive possibilities for the future and generate the emotional heat you need to create them.

The word "for-give" means to "give again as before," to act as though the offense never happened which sounds superhuman when all you're feeling is, "No way! He was totally in the wrong!" But as a colleague once told us, "Forgiving doesn't free the other person. It frees you."

Holding on to an offense keeps you stuck in the past, carting the burden of your anger around with you everywhere, reliving the pain every time some remark or circumstance reminds you of what happened. And the fact is, every single one of us has not one, but a long list of offenses we suffered at the hands (and mouths) of yet another long list of perpetrators. At any moment, we could whip out our lists and feel really bad. We could rank our offenses from least to most upsetting. We could even compare notes and decide who ought to be angrier or more indignant.

But that wouldn't change anything.

It would only renew the anger we felt when the offenses happened.

We'd feel lousy all over again.

There would be no chance of a fresh start in a new relationship with the offenders.

And the offenses would live forever.

Forgive, and we can let go of the anger and offense, be free of it for good and ready to move on to better things, unburdened by the past.

Right about now, you're remembering a particular hurt or offense and thinking, "Impossible! After what she did? No way!" but like optimism, forgiveness isn't a feeling; it's a decision followed by deliberate action, and that decision may or may not be supported by your feelings. Once again, just because you don't _feel_ forgiving doesn't mean you can't _be_ forgiving.

Give yourself a break. Don't wait for your feelings to change to drop the heavy burden of old offenses. Make the choice to forgive—_for your own sake_—and just think of what you'll do

Working Wisdom

Forgive... but don't forget

Though it's often coupled with the word, "forgive" doesn't mean "forget" and put yourself in the identical situation with a repeat offender, knowing the same thing is likely to happen, and then being frustrated or disappointed once again when it does.

Forgiveness doesn't mean trusting someone who's been repeatedly undependable, unpredictable, or disloyal in the past. And it doesn't mean allowing yourself to be taken advantage of, or accepting blame for something you're truly not accountable for, especially when doing so will tarnish your reputation.

Let go of the offense—stop thinking about it and don't relive it by discussing it with others—then graciously keep your distance from any repeat offenders.

Working Wisdom

Bullet proof

A colleague on fire with her newfound skill of High Possibility Thinking once told us: "I had to stick my foot in my mouth a few times, get shut down by a prospect who wasn't interested, lose the sale, the customer, and the key employee during our busy season before I could develop positive expectation.

"It's easy to be optimistic when everything is going well. Where's the challenge in that? But when I learned how to expect the best in the face of obstacles—to see them as opportunities—not only did I grow, I bullet-proofed my business."

"Obstacle as opportunity" transcends the clichés about "seeing the bright side" or the "glass being half full." It's a powerful and proven strategy for breaking through to new heights of success.

(continued on page 63)

with all that energy freshly channeled into activities that are future-focused and positive.

Stay connected

When you start to use asset-based thinking and language at work, your colleagues may find the change in you strange and unsettling. Frankly, they may not welcome the new you, and you may be tempted to go back to old negative patterns rather than risk losing friends.

Some people take the opposite approach: instead of returning to old patterns, they start to preach, boldly proclaiming that they've seen the light of positive expectation (which of course makes them emotionally and professionally superior) and alienating everyone within hearing distance. The poor person who approaches them for a heart-to-heart about something that's troubling him might be dismissed with a thoughtless, "Oh, that's not true! I used to think like that once. Not anymore! You should try to be more positive!"

Still a third group will begin to run from tough situations or to act like Prince or Princess Positive, as if they can't even *hear* anything negative. If you ever start to think, "I'm working on

being more positive so I don't want to be involved with negative people or situations," catch yourself. There is no such place, and real Positive Power is the ability to be in a negative situation but respond positively to it.

As you ingrain the habit of positive expectation in your own life, keep your relationships intact and strong. When a colleague expresses a fear, frustration, or low expectation, acknowledge it before moving the conversation onto more positive ground:

- "I totally get where you're coming from on this. You're right to be concerned."

- "Sounds like a lot to handle."

- "I've been there, so I really understand."

- "That's an excellent point."

- "That's an important question."

- "You're not alone. Lots of people have the same concern."

Then, when it feels right, suggest a positive next step:

- "One idea I had that you might want to try is…"

- "Something I've seen work in a similar situation is…"

(continued from page 62)

As our colleague bottom-lined, it's the challenges—not the successes or the routines—that produce our growth spurts. No one is motivated to take giant steps in easy times. But when the going gets tough, we're searching for solutions, open to new ideas and strategies.

That means that each time you stumble, speak out of turn, blow it, or lose out, you're at your most—not least—powerful, surprising sometimes even yourself with your strength and resilience. You embrace the new ideas, put them to work, and come back with new insights and victories. You've raised the bar on yourself. Your breakthrough isn't far off.

For more on the topic of using obstacles as opportunities, you may also want to see Part 2 of our book Hot Situations, Cool Heads: How to Thrive When Conflict Arrives. *You can get a copy by visiting us at www.breakthroughskills.com.*

- "I think there's enough positive potential to give it a try…"

- "You might want to think about…"

- "I have a colleague who might be able to help you with that…"

- "Maybe you could try looking at the issue in another way…"

Keeping the mood light is another strategy for staying connected to colleagues as you make this important change in your outlook and attitude. If someone teases, "Well, would you listen to Mr. Pos-i-tive!" try a smile and a breezy comment like:

- "That's Smith to you! No seriously, it doesn't have to seem so bad."

- "I know, I know…it's the new shoes/outfit/cough medicine talking. But really, what if we just tried…"

- "Okay, call me crazy, but I really think we can make this work…"

- "Just wanted to move the project along, so we don't get bogged down in the same issues again…"

When you subtly introduce your colleagues to a more positive way of thinking and talking, they won't think you've gone off and had a personality transplant. Instead, all they'll notice is that they feel better—more hopeful and inspired—when you're in the room.

Positive Power

Notes

— Take Five —

Strong, stretched, and centered

It's tough to think hopeful, positive thoughts when you're tired or run down. Set yourself up for success by staying healthy, strong, and vibrant. Exercise regularly, eat right, and get enough sleep.

Exercise

With just 24 hours in the day, and only 16 of them waking, it may seem impossible to include exercise in your weekly routine, but include it you must, and it must be consistent. From strength, stamina, and flexibility to stress reduction and disease prevention, exercise is without equal in its ability to improve your health and outlook. Regular exercise even helps you sleep better.

Here is an example of a simple three-part formula for a balanced exercise regimen we call Sweat, Strength, and Stretch:

> **Sweat** requires 20 to 30 minutes of aerobic activity. Fitness walking is a great choice. For the cost of a good pair of walking shoes, you can exercise anywhere and get a great cardiovascular workout, especially if you pump your arms, with minimal stress on your joints. Other aerobic options

include swimming, cycling, jogging, and aerobic classes or DVDs you can follow at home.

Strength work (lifting weights, doing pushups, sit-ups, or any other type of muscle strengthening exercise) is an extremely important component of any exercise regimen. This type of training, often called "resistance" training, strengthens your muscles and helps build bone density. Strong muscles protect your joints, reshape your body, and actually burn calories, even when you're standing still!

Stretching, a third essential element of a fitness program, keeps you toned and limber, prevents injuries, and enables you to move freely and more quickly. Flexibility work through simple stretches, yoga, or Pilates™ exercise protects you from muscle tears and aches—including disabling back pains—and enables you to move more comfortably and fluidly throughout the day.

Important!

Before beginning any exercise program or changing your diet, be sure to check with your health care professional to be certain that you needn't limit your physical activity in any way, and that any dietary changes you'd like to make are appropriate for you.

Diet

Next, equally (if not more) important is diet. We can exercise week after week, but a steady diet devoid of vitamins and fiber will drag us down. We know that eating refined sugar and flour in great quantities, not eating enough protein (women are famous for this), drinking diet soda (ditto—the waiter never has to wonder who gets the diet soda), and using sugar substitutes, all make us feel drained and agitated. If your nutritional day consists of coffee with a muffin or bagel for breakfast, a sandwich and chips or a slice of pizza for lunch, then more coffee and maybe a mid-afternoon pick-me-up of a candy bar or yet another bag of chips, and for dinner, a serving (or two) of meat, white potatoes or rice and a blanched-to-oblivion vegetable plus dessert, you're not getting anywhere near the nutrition you need to feel good and think clearly.

It's a new day, and time to begin making better choices about what you eat.

The very good news is that eating right is simple. Make an effort to eat a breakfast with some type of whole grain (for example, oats, shredded wheat, or 12-grain bread), and a protein like an egg or cup of plain yogurt. For lunch, have a salad with tuna or chicken, seeds or nuts, or chunks of low-fat cheese. Skip the high-fat dressing in favor of a vinaigrette, and have a slice or two of whole grain bread. For dinner, reduce your portion of meat, chicken, or fish, have just a cup of brown rice or a sweet potato or yam for fiber, and add a huge salad or serving of steamed vegetables. A few times a week, try a vegetarian meal: beans and rice, tofu and vegetables, soup, fruit, salad with nuts and sprouts, vegetarian chili and chips…the options are endless, and delicious.

Between meals, drink plenty of water. Get yourself a quart-sized jug, and fill it in the morning. Finish it by lunch time. Do the same for the afternoon. Between meals, opt for fruit instead of junk. For munchies, you can find healthful alternatives for everything you crave. Rather than reaching for cookies or ice cream, satisfy your sweet tooth with a low fat granola bar, a banana dipped in raisins, or a baked apple with cinnamon. Keep a supply of frozen berries at home and put them in the microwave just long enough to soften them, drizzle honey on top for another sweet treat that's also packed with healthful antioxidants. Instead of greasy, salty chips, try low fat, low- or no-salt pretzels or corn chips with salsa. These are all great snack choices that have whole grains and natural (slower burning) sugars that satisfy you longer and also provide fiber and vitamins. Learn to drink your coffee or tea without sugar and opt for seltzer over soda, even (especially) diet soda.

Reduce the stress on your heart—and your psyche—by keeping your weight at a level that enables you to feel healthy and physically comfortable. Don't overeat, but don't starve either.

Take the time to shop smart for clothes: spend time choosing comfortable, but still fashion-conscious shoes and clothes for the office so you can concentrate on your work and not how much your feet hurt or how tight your collar is.

Rest and balance

Get enough sleep. In this overworked, constantly overtired society, precious rest is too rare. Turn off the TV, put the novel down, leave the clothes in the basket until tomorrow. Sleep is more important. Don't eat or drink caffeine after dinner so you can sleep more comfortably.

Finally, balance your days and weeks: in addition to work, make time for your family, friendships, and spiritual well being. Stop and smell the roses, but also clip a few, put them in some water, place them on a table, make a mug of coffee, call a friend or sit down with a good book or magazine…and breathe.

Part 2: Proactive Power

You set the agenda

The word "proactive" seems to pop up everywhere in business today. It's become quite the buzzword, used to mean everything from simple planning to good decision-making to risk management. Being proactive simply means preparing to succeed at whatever you're doing: tackling a project, searching for a dream job, expanding your business, or recovering from a blunder or the loss of a star employee. It's the deliberate actions you take to squeeze every drop of positive potential out of a good situation or squelch the negative potential of a not-so-good one.

> "Look and you will find it. What is unsought will go undetected."
>
> —Sophocles,
> Ancient Greek playwright

Squeeze or squelch, the common element is *potential.* To be proactive is to manage this potential to your advantage, making the most of a positive event (planning who will be there, what you'll say, what you'll prepare in advance), and controlling a negative one (making an extra call to get support from an influential colleague, carefully planning the changes you want to set in motion).

It's no surprise that a concept this powerful has gotten such wide play. Proactive thinking gives teams and even entire businesses an almost unfair advantage over competitors who sit back wait-and-see style before they act. On a more personal level, being proactive puts *you* in control. When you take the deliberate steps to manage the potential outcome in a situation to your advantage, *you set the agenda.* Rather than having to react to random circumstances or someone else's goals—in effect, giving your power away—you're out ahead, predetermining the best possible outcome and working hard to make it happen.

Sounds pretty straightforward, and it is, in theory. But when we began to plan this section on **Proactive Power,** we got hit by a tidal wave of how-to's for proactive thinking and action. And we had yet to add the one type of proactive thinking we consider essential gear for breakthrough-bound people.

Not so simple any more.

So here's our plan: in the pages that follow, we'll cover a range of ways you can use **Proactive Power** in your work life. Then we'll wrap this section by giving you the secret of the most powerful form of proactive thinking for people determined to reach the next level in their careers or businesses.

Here goes.

Proactive Power enables you to…

Prevent hiccups

As a routine step to prepare for an important event, conversation, project, or meeting, set aside some uninterruptible time, sharpen a pencil, and make a list of everything that could go wrong: every glitch, mishap, and/or malfunction you can think of. Then, make a "just-in-case" plan for each one.

We asked a few colleagues to share with us the "what-ifs" they typically plan for. Here's what they told us:

- "Be sure you have a 'Plan B' if your technology fails. For example, have a backup projector or bring printed copies of your presentation slides in case the projector is older than your laptop, you forget your thumb drive, or don't have internet access, and you're too nervous and self-conscious to fix the problem."

- "When you're using a certain consultant or supplier for the first time, start with a small, low-risk order or project so you can see how they work and the quality of their products. Never risk getting acquainted on a large, visible project…just in case it doesn't go well."

- "Leave for every meeting *much* earlier than you need to. If a meeting is especially important, plan enough time to get a flat tire, fix it, get yourself cleaned up, and still arrive ten minutes early. And never leave just enough time to get there when the meeting is scheduled to begin. I speak from experience on this one."

- "Prepare for an important conversation by practicing the names of key people, so they roll off your tongue easily, especially if there are foreign or unfamiliar names you need to know. Never risk mispronouncing someone's name in a high stakes situation, or any situation for that matter. People can get amazingly insulted by this, and that really puts you at a disadvantage."

- "Invite more than one expert on an important topic to a key meeting in case the person you're depending on doesn't show."

- "Give a new employee specific instructions—rather than general suggestions—on how to complete an important task or project. Then, check for understanding: 'Does this make sense to you? Do you understand what you need to do?' This also applies to an employee you've had trouble with. Don't give them the latitude to decide what to do because you're asking for a headache. Be clear and specific so you can help them do well, get some kudos, and hopefully break out of a bad pattern."

- "Know your audience, whether you're talking during a meeting, giving a sales presentation, or having a one-on-one conversation. Don't think about what you want to say. Think about what they need to know. Try to anticipate and prepare for their reactions: what questions are they likely to ask you? What concerns are you likely to encounter? How will you respond to put the person's mind at ease?"

- "If you're giving a presentation, prepare a question you'd like to be asked and keep it in your back pocket. At the end, when you say, 'Are there any questions?' if no one raises a hand, you can say, 'A question I'm often asked is…' or 'Many times people want to know…' This makes you sound more in command of the situation and keeps you from having to deal with that uncomfortable silence that happens so often when you ask for questions. It also gives your audience time to think of their questions. Lots of times, as I'm answering my own question, I see hands start to go up."

- "Three musts when you're visiting a client or prospect:

  1. bring lunch money!

  2. never forget you're a guest; be on your best behavior with everyone within a 10 mile radius of the building (you never know who's an employee).

  3. plan and mentally rehearse some small talk about your trip to the building or a recent sports event so you're never caught with nothing to talk about."

- "If you want to suggest an idea that's progressive or edgy, share it first with a colleague and get some constructive feedback. Make changes as needed in either the content or your planned delivery of the idea (timing, setting, etc.) so your audience is receptive."

- "Keep business cards with you, and always have your 30-second 'elevator speech' fresh in your mind so you sound super-smooth when someone asks you what you do."

Planning for these and other contingencies is loaded with advantages: first, it keeps you calm and focused so you can approach whatever challenge you're facing with more confidence. It also keeps others calm, so they can concentrate and not be agitated by the mishap or distracted by your discomfort over it. And planning for hiccups also shows that you're experienced enough to know the things that *could* go wrong, and smart enough to be ready for them. One of the highest compliments you can get at work is that you're smooth under pressure. "What a pro!" they'll think. "A flat tire on the way here, and still she's on time and totally prepared to meet with us!"

Working Wisdom

Watch your proxy

Stretch a budget

"How much does a car cost?"

"What kind of car?"

"Just a car, any car."

"Depends."

"On what?"

"Lots of things: the make, model, accessories, and other things for a new car. For a used car, the age, mileage, history."

"Okay, if you think about all those things, how much does a car cost?"

"Why do you want to know?"

"I'm thinking about getting one."

This episode of *Adventures in Parenting* was brought to you by 10-year-old Jason, a friend's son.

We can all be a little Jason-like when we're spending money. We zero in on cost without thinking of value or what we'll get for what we're spending. This is the one reason every consulting novice learns never to quote a price for a project before explaining their experience with that type of project, the steps involved, and the resources they'll use to complete the work. This is to help the prospect understand not just the cost but the value they would receive and make an informed buying decision.

For example, the fee quoted by a consultant with 15 years of experience who has handled a specific type of project before, who will take extra steps to ensure it's done right and has access to a host of resources and experts can't be compared apples-to-apples to a price quoted by someone with just three years experience, who hasn't handled this type of project before and who either doesn't know or can't explain the steps involved. The same rule applies to any sales situation. Your turbocharged metallic widgets with the lifetime guarantee can't be compared to the plastic prefab widgets in the shop down the street. Yours will cost more, but offer more value.

Money isn't the only resource we spend without enough regard for value. In fact, we're probably even less careful about the value of our time. We waste time online, on the phone, procrastinating, searching for files, struggling with tasks when help is available…and don't even get us started on the time we waste in meetings!

Our local print shop posted a sign that reads:

> *You can have it **fast**. You can have it **good**.*
> *You can have it **cheap**. Pick two."*

In other words, you can get your print job done fast and good, but not cheap. Or good and cheap, but not fast. Or fast and cheap, but not good. As two of life's most important resources, time and money work together in the value equation.

Business sometimes substitutes the word "efficiency" for value, meaning the more you get for your money or the more you accomplish in a given period of time, the more efficient you are which is the same as getting greater value out of these key resources.

All this preamble to make an essential point about **Proactive Power:** as costs rise and the business world picks up speed, getting the greatest value out of time and money can be the razor-thin margin between success and failure. Use **Proactive Power** to become a high value player with your time and money, and watch your potential reach new heights.

So, how do you stretch a dollar...or an hour?

Money

- If you're using an outside vendor for a project:
    - Get three estimates so you can compare cost <u>and</u> value before you decide to make a sizable purchase.
    - Set aside enough uninterruptible time to scrutinize a contract before you sign to be certain the terms are balanced and make sense for your team or business.
    - Set (and stick to!) a project budget.
    - Watch expenses carefully.
    - Establish an open dialogue on the topic of fees and expenses with the vendor you choose. Share any specific concerns you have about the budget, under- score important contract terms (e.g., exceeding the budget is NOT an option, extra expenses must be approved in advance), and in general, ask for the vendor's help in keeping costs under control.

- Negotiate volume discounts with any suppliers with whom you do a lot of business.

- Ask vendors you've used repeatedly whether they can give you more favorable rates based on your long-standing relationship. (Don't be shy—just ask!)

- Take full advantage of prompt payer discounts any vendor or supplier offers.

- Look for more economical options whenever you can ("Does the package really need to be sent by messenger, or would overnight be fine?" "Do we need to send a separate mailing, or can we piggyback on a mailing we've already planned to do this year?").

- Insist that every expense be an investment that helps you build your career or business into something greater.

Time

- Delegate effectively:

  - Let go of work that doesn't offer you or your company real value or tasks that could be done more effectively or at lower cost by someone else or through automation. This includes pet projects, rote tasks, and time-gobbling jobs that prevent you from tackling more high profile work that could move your career or business forward.

  - Be familiar with the skills and experience levels of the people resources (employees and contractors) available to you: Who is super detail-oriented? Who has experience with targeted marketing campaigns? Who knows the magazine publishing industry? and hand out assignments based on people's strengths and workloads.

- Shorten your learning curve. Rather than struggle for a week trying to solve a problem on your own, ask an expert. (This actually does more than save time. It forges new relationships with experienced people on positive terms. Everyone loves to be recognized as an expert and asked for advice.)

- Look into new tools and methods for working smarter and getting more done in less time. What new software is available to streamline your work and make you more efficient? How about books, articles, and websites? Online or classroom workshops?

- Opt for online books and self-study courses rather than classroom training, which tends to be the most expensive option, both in terms of time and dollar outlay.

- Get organized! Take a trip to an office supply store and treat yourself to colored file folders, tabs, markers, labels, sticky notes, and any clip or gadget you can use to organize the bazillion pieces of paper that record your life. And don't stop with paper. Organize your books, supplies, cabinets, clothes, shoes…everything. Put supplies you use most often in an easy access spot. Group your books by subject. Toss dried out markers and twisted paper clips. Donate any work clothes you haven't worn in a year to Goodwill Missions or Dress for Success, then rearrange your closet by matching outfits so mornings are a no-brainer. Just imagine the time you'd save if you never had to search for your best blue blazer, a credit card statement, or the White Out® again.

Flex some "what if...?" and "what's next...?" muscles

Every manager and client handing out work has a secret wish, and it goes something like this: "Please do the job right, and after that, PLEASE do more than I'm asking you to do."

Regardless of the type of work you do, taking a job further makes you more valuable. This means asking:

What's next?

- Thinking of the next step, and the next.
- Adding ideas from your experience working for other companies or clients.
- Identifying other projects or programs in the company that would benefit from the work you're doing.

What if?

- Thinking creatively about the steps you're taking to streamline the process or make it work better in some other way.
- Involving another person or team whose expertise will improve the quality of the work.
- Even telling your manager or client that there's a better way to accomplish the same end and going into that conversation thoroughly prepared to talk about it. (For obvious reasons, this is not a discussion to have at the last minute, but rather in ADVANCE of the date you're supposed to have the work done!)

…and any other way you can make the finished product better and get the work done faster.

For example:

> "What if we include the Marketing team in the June meeting? They can probably tell us how to talk about the benefits of our idea to the Product Manager. Let's see if they're available."

"Let's find out how much we can save next year if we consolidate all our office supply purchases with one vendor. We'll start with a list of suppliers to consider."

"Last year, the client said she wished we had more time to plan the annual Sales Meeting. If we start a month earlier, we'll be able to plan more breakout discussions and maybe even include the European team via satellite. Let's put a timeline together now."

Flexing your "What if?" and "What's next?" muscles makes you more valuable, but it also shows that you enjoy and are excited about what you do, believe that added quality matters, are invested in the work and the success of the team or business, and frankly that you just plain old give a darn. As a plus, we know from personal experience as well as from clients that flexing these muscles on a regular basis prevents boredom and makes work fun. "I've got to do this job 8 hours a day," we overheard one employee in a busy medical practice tell another. "Why wouldn't I want to find ways to make it fun?"

In our world of business communications, there's nothing worse than a person who does what we tell them—and only what we tell them. This is especially tough on us when we need help in an area where we have no expertise or no time to concentrate on the task to do it right. Graphic design and bookkeeping are two great examples. If the person we hire to design a book, brochure, poster, or anything else does only what we tell them, without challenging us with new ideas and adding their expertise, we're sunk. We know what we like when we see it, but we don't have enough visual talent to ask for it specifically. We're trusting the designer's expertise to make that image materialize for us. And gosh, if we ask for something ridiculous, tell us! Please don't ever send it to us with a note that reads, "Here's what you asked for."

Ditto our business finances. We want the person we hire as our bookkeeper to be first and foremost accurate and honest, but also aggressive with our money. How can we save on expenses? What do we need to do to monitor our contracts better? What's the best way to organize our files so we can find every piece of paper when we need it? Are we sticking to our budgets?

We want the people we hire to do the job right AND set us up for longer-term success. And what's true for our small business is true for businesses everywhere. It's been years since companies promoted people for doing what they were told. Fresh ideas and initiative are among today's most sought-after qualities.

Here are some questions to help you flex your "what if?" and "what's next?" muscles:

- "What's the best result for our team or business? Are we doing everything we can to bring this about?"
- "How can we pick up momentum toward our goal? What steps can we take to:
    - save time or money?
    - create more energy and excitement for the goal?
    - get additional support from influential people?"
- "What next steps would:
    - keep moving this effort along and make sure it doesn't stall?
    - show my manager/team/client/customer that I've got the long-term success of this program in sight?"

Working Wisdom

Satisfy unspoken needs

We once got this advice from an ace salesperson: "The secret of sales success is simple: if the customer is buying shoes, ask if they have enough socks." In other words, satisfy their unspoken needs.

Think: what complementary or follow-on product, service, or information can you recommend to a customer that they either don't know they need or don't realize you offer?

For example, if they're buying a book, ask whether they've read the author's other works.

If you're delivering customer survey data, ask if they might be interested in comparative information from other businesses in their industry.

In addition to increasing your sales, satisfying unspoken needs is a proactive practice that helps you project the image of an expert who understands the full breadth of a customer's needs. You also build rapport with customers who appreciate your recommendations for useful items they didn't think of.

...all while proactively giving the customer more value or a more complete solution to his needs.

- "What is my boss/client/customer most likely to ask me to do next?"

- "Which teammates or colleagues would be willing/able to brainstorm next steps with me?"

- "Which executive/s in my company can help me create interest and support by endorsing my project or goal?"

- "If I didn't have a boss—or if I were the boss—what would I do next?"

- "If I were running this project or initiative, at this point, I'd want the person working for me to..."

- "How are other teams or businesses treating this issue? What's working for them? How can I apply these ideas as I decide what to do next?"

- "If the customer is buying [product/service], what else do we offer that she might also need?"

- "Beyond what I have to do, what more can I do? What's the extra 2 percent I can do to take this effort from good to excellent? What additional fact can I add or phone call can I make to check for more information or stronger corroboration?"

When you think this way, the people you work for and with don't have to. You save them from having to worry about every idea, detail, and next step...and do they ever appreciate that.

Follow through on feedback

Fair or unfair, reputation is the basis people use to find merit in us. A positive reputation opens doors to opportunities, new relationships, and new business. A negative one creates limits.

What's your reputation? What do the influential people in your work life think about your goals, performance, and potential? Knowing is a must because when you're aware of your reputation, you can fix misperceptions about your goals ("I didn't know you were interested in Marketing. I always thought you wanted to run a sales team/stay on the East Coast/work for Celine one day!") and clear up any confusion about your expertise ("I never knew you had an engineering degree/lived in Singapore for a year/spoke fluent French!").

A caveat

In sensitive or high-stakes situations, make sure you test the waters before moving ahead with any new ideas or next steps.

Or go directly to your boss or client and say, "Here's where we are. I've thought through some next steps and wanted to run them by you for your opinion/approval so I can make any adjustments before moving ahead."

Don't wait to find out by accident that people think you want to stay in sales when you're really interested in public relations. Or that you're a great systems technician who's also a good marketer, when you really want them to think that you're a great marketer who's also a good systems technician. Or that you're still a copywriter when you've expanded your services and are now offering strategic communications planning.

Ask the influential people in your work life for feedback and then follow through on what you hear in ways that are visible to the person who gave you the input:

- Radiate readiness and interest in input from your colleagues. Listen fully to any feedback they volunteer—even if it's not positive. Don't dismiss it or begin to defend yourself. Instead, respond with:
  - "Thanks for your honesty."
  - "I'll definitely look into that."
  - "I see where you're coming from. Do you have some time to talk more about that idea?"

- When you ask for someone's feedback, let them know you truly want their honest, no-holds-barred opinion of your ideas, contributions, reputation, strengths, or performance on a key project: "Please be frank with me. I really respect your opinion."

- Pick your timing. If you want feedback on your presentation, ask for it immediately afterward, or the next day when the memory is still fresh. And, needless to say, avoid asking someone who's overburdened with work or deadlines.

- Opt for informal. Rather than try to pin someone down for an hour-long talk, invite them to lunch or coffee and ask for their feedback on the way. Or wrap up a phone call with someone whose opinion matters with a simple, "I wanted to be sure I asked you whether that summary I sent was helpful?"

- Keep a few open-ended questions in your back pocket to use when the moment seems right:
  - "Would you tell me what you found helpful about my presentation?"

- "When you have a minute, would you let me know what more I could do to support you?"

- "I'd love to know the top two reasons you buy from me."

- "I've built my business on our reputation for quality. Would you tell me what you consider my company's best product/service?"

Thank the person for their input. Then filter out what's truly helpful and empowering and decide how you'll use it.

Don't miss an essential point here: you won't always get usable feedback and certainly not everything you hear will lift your spirits. But gathering practical feedback is only half the goal.

The *Showcase* section of any of our *Breakthrough Journals*© is a great resource on how to let someone see you've created positive change. Visit *www. breakthroughskills.com* to get a copy.

The other half is showing that you've got a set of qualities that positively shout growth and breakthrough potential:

- an openness to new ideas

- approachability

- the intention to constantly improve

- respect for and connection to your colleagues

…all of which you broadcast just by being open to ideas and ready to take action on them.

Shake things up a bit

When was the last time you felt the thrill of reaching for a stretch goal or the tingle of nerves at trying something new?

How about the last time you suggested a radical idea or raised your hand to volunteer for a high risk or high profile project?

Too long?

Granted, predictability is important, and we tend to become more conservative about risk taking as we advance in our careers and have more to conserve. But if the balance of your work life has shifted way over to comfort and routine, there's a good chance you're missing opportunities, not to mention the sheer know-you're-alive joy of an adrenalin rush.

Shake things up by taking on a thrilling challenge, and you get all this and more. You also get used to handling the unpredictable, meeting new people, adapting to unique situations, and thinking in terms of possibilities ("What can I do with this new situation?" "Who else can help my team?" "What would give us more momentum?"). These are great muscles to flex, not only for your breakthrough quest, but for your confidence and self esteem too.

Give yourself the gift of circumstances that let you—and everyone else—see all that you're capable of:

- Make a phone call you've been putting off. Then make three more.

- Arrange that high-stakes meeting you thought about last week.

- Volunteer to work on a task force or special project team. Once assigned to the team, ask for a leadership role.

- Commit to achieving a stretch goal: a raise, bonus, or promotion in the next 12 months, a new client you used to think was out of your league, a sales milestone that seems out of reach. Do some research and build a detailed action plan for reaching it (including the people and resources (books, websites, courses, etc.) that can help catalyze your success).

- Commit to a new project or stretch goal for your team or business: How about 50 new clients in the next 24 months, or the latest contact management software on everyone's desktop by yearend? Maybe a new Careers page on the company's website to attract new employees or an e-commerce store...

- Go to a professional association meeting this month and introduce yourself to two (make that 10!) new people.

- Ask someone you don't ordinarily socialize with to lunch. Do this once a week.

- Take a course or sign up for a lecture series on a topic outside your area of expertise. Summarize what you learn and share it with your colleagues.

- Go to a local Toastmasters meeting and make a presentation.

Add a few of your own ideas to our list, then make them a habit. Accepting new opportunities and challenges sends a clear message to your colleagues—and to you—that you're adaptable, open, and ready to stretch your experience and knowledge into new arenas and up to new heights.

Keep an ear to the ground

Change happens. Faster by the day. Just try visiting a dealership if you haven't bought a car in a few years. Now you can push a button, and someone sitting halfway around the country will send help. Lost? Input an address and you've got a full color map in front of you with a bright red line that shows you how to get there. Thirsty? Just grab a cold soda from the built-in refrigerator. Kids restless on those long drives?

Let them watch a movie on the DVD screen. How about a subscription to satellite radio and TV? No problem!

And you can bet that next year, cars will have even more bells, whistles and conveniences. Why? Because the serious players in the automotive industry don't kid themselves about how competitive it is. They spend billions of dollars to research consumer needs, plan safety enhancements, and press forward on advances in fuel economy and alternative power sources to keep the planet green. They don't stand still because they know if they do, they'll be eating another car company's dust.

Some tough love from us to you: do not think for a minute that you can stand still and succeed. No matter what you do, for whom, or where, you've got to refresh your knowledge and skills constantly. Not only will this discipline help you deliver consistently exceptional work, it will make you the go-to person when the team needs someone with vision. On a more personal level, staying fresh keeps your energy up and makes work exciting and fun.

So keep an ear to the ground. Be aware of trends in your field, including changes that affect your specific job (sales, office management, event planning, IT) and the type of company you do it for (transportation, HR consulting, commercial construction, real estate management). Join professional and industry groups and subscribe to publications that report on events and new developments in your industry. What's hot today? What's coming? How are other people and companies taking advantage of these changes? What technology is on the horizon? What skills will you need in the future? What courses or books will help you prepare?

Look for changes in your company's performance reviews. What categories are dropping off the form, and what new ones are showing up? Why? What will you have to do in the future to earn top ratings on your next review?

If your company has an awards program, who's being recognized and for what achievements? If your industry or profession recognizes outstanding individuals every year, what can you do to earn similar kudos?

Know the answers to questions like:

- "What's my company's top priority for this month/quarter/year? How are we doing?"
- "Is my team capable of supporting these priorities? Am I?"
- "If not, what do I/we need to start doing differently?"
- "How can we set that in motion right away?"

If you run a business, watch for changes in your key markets:

- What new software or hardware is available? How can you use these to make your front- or back-end operation more efficient?
- What new competitors are entering your field? What are they offering that you aren't?
- Should you consider adding to your products or services? Specializing in a specific area or two?
- What's the next big thing, the next breakthrough, in your industry? What steps can you take now so you're ready to take maximum advantage of it?

Avoid slippage

It can happen when you're not paying attention, or when you've been doing the same job for a while. It can happen when you delegate a job but neglect to give the person complete instructions. We've seen it happen when a consultant gets too comfortable with a client and begins to think, "After all these years as my client, Joe's become a friend of mine. I don't have to worry about every little detail. He'll understand." (Wanna bet?)

Slippage. It happens when you don't check the one detail you always carefully managed. Maybe it's Friday, and it's been a long week. It's not going to make that much of a difference, right? Or maybe you just wave off that final fact check you did on the last report. Oh, it's probably fine. No need to sweat it.

Slippage happens when you neglect the extra two percent of effort you always put in because the timing on this project is so tight. It happens after the call you don't bother to make, the "cc" you omit. After the "Oops, I probably should have included Joann on that distribution list. Oh well, whatever."

You get the idea. Whether the word is being used in engine mechanics, investing, or personal performance, slippage means a loss of momentum in terms of both forward movement and power.

The real danger of slippage is that when you see that the ground doesn't open up and swallow you after a small oversight or misstep, slowly, "less than" becomes acceptable: less than excellent, slightly behind schedule, not quite well planned. You can get used to it. It's not so bad, in fact, it makes your life easier because you spend less time sweating the details.

But beware. Once you get in this groove, small misses and minor mistakes start to add up, hurting your reputation and holding you back. Don't go there. Decide that you will deliver the same level of excellence on every effort, every day: keep appointments, return calls, meet with people, check your facts, take next steps, and do the extra two percent that takes a project from good to excellent. Catch even the smallest mistakes and omissions, and invest the effort to fix them fast.

Set goals

Goals are the ultimate in proactive thinking because they plot the home runs of your work life and how you will hit them. They also keep you focused by helping you tell the difference between pothole-sized problems and mere bumps in the road. When you look at an event in the context of your goals, you can see just how much energy and attention it's worth.

Goals also let you get out of fire-fighting mode in your daily work. Stop running around, take out your list of goals, and stare at them for a few minutes. As you distinguish the short-term fires demanding so much of your attention from the long-term goals of your life, you get your bearings and feel your blood pressure return to normal.

Goals make it easy to organize and prioritize your time. The amount of time you choose to spend on a specific activity—the priority it receives on a given day—should be in proportion to the activity's ability to activate or advance your most important goals.

Set daily, weekly, monthly, and annual goals for yourself. They can be general guidelines or specific, measurable achievements. Just make sure they're meaningful and motivating to you.

Examples:

- "More family time."

- "Increase sales 10 percent this year."

- "Don't procrastinate!"

For a great goal-setting exercise, see **Part 5: My Goals** of the Breakthrough Skills resource: *The THINK! Workbook.* Visit *www. breakthroughskills.com* to get your copy.

- "Make in-person contact with 20 clients/prospects per month."

- "Finish all quarterly reports on time or early."

- "Hold monthly all-staff meetings on progress toward financial targets."

- "Get promoted to Marketing Director."

- "Sell the most coveted account for my company."

- "Get organized!"

- "Have coffee with the CEO."

- "Make two sales presentations a month."

Choose to respond

We have a secret passion for cooking shows on cable TV. Not long ago, we watched four students compete for a chance to run their own restaurant. The atmosphere was competitive, but the young contestants were surprisingly mature and supportive of each other, with one exception. One of them, clearly younger than the rest and maybe in a little over his head, was self-concerned and harsh, and he refused to lend a hand when one of his fellow contestants needed help.

When his own dish flopped, something interesting happened. The young man who had taken the brunt of his rudeness and self involvement said quietly to himself, "I'm not that guy." It wasn't clear whether he meant, "I'm not going to lower myself to his level by reacting to him," or "I'm not the type of person who will give him back what he's given me." Regardless, his decision not to react was a choice to create the type of situation that reflected who *he* was and what *his* goals were. It was a choice to define the moment his way. He helped his colleague salvage the dish and said a great deal about himself and his professionalism in the process. He also won the contest.

Use this example and create the career or business you want—one that reflects your values and destinations—rather than one built out of your reactions to other people's decisions and actions.

Whatever you're experiencing, take a moment to think about your plans and dreams for the future. With these top of mind, choose a reaction.

Affirmations—like the one the young man in this story used ("I'm not that guy")—can help. If you feel yourself rising to react in an unproductive or uncharacteristic way to someone's bad behavior, find a private spot, sit or stand up straight, and in a clear voice tell yourself:

- "I can absolutely handle this."

- "What matters most is not what happened, but what I do next."

- "I will not get sidetracked by this."

- "I'm proud of my achievements and have faith in my abilities."

- "I can turn this into a positive."

- "I will choose to keep my cool and walk away from this situation with my reputation and dignity intact."

Manage expectations

She knocked on our door in the Spring of 1994 to hand-deliver her resume in response to our ad for a Marketing Manager. Her genuine warmth and high energy told us this was someone worth talking to. We invited her in, and ended up hiring her that day.

In the seven years Florence worked for Morris Communications, she brought decades of experience, fresh ideas, and a remark-able ability to set healthy boundaries. Florence would take a walk every day for 20 minutes at lunchtime, in rain, shine, bliz-zard, hurricane, sweltering heat, or monsoon. It never varied, and it was never skipped. She would also leave at 5:00. Every day. She did not bring work home and did not come in early. Ever. "As I've gotten older," she once confided, "my time has become much more precious. I've learned to value even the minutes."

But she was always on time ("If I'm ever late," she once joked, "call the police because something's really wrong."), and she never missed a deadline. She was never in a bad mood, and her creativity and class were absolutely consistent.

You might think this kind of rigidity about time was an annoy-ance or even a liability to us in a client-driven business where it isn't at all unusual for a client to call at 4:30 with questions or changes that need to be made in a matter of hours. But it wasn't. Quite the opposite—her utter reliability was reassur-ing, and made it easy to plan her work.

We're not advocating leaving at 5:00 or never starting early, but notice what happens when you manage expectations proactively. The people you work with and for come to appreciate your consistency and integrity. They can relax knowing that coming from you, "yes" means "yes," and "no" means "no."

Some examples of this proactive practice in action:

- If your time is already stretched, tell the client who asks for a report by Tuesday that you can have it done by Friday. If you're able to finish by Tuesday, the client will be delighted. If not, he'll be satisfied when it arrives on Friday. Delighted or satisfied...but never disappointed.

For more on managing expectations, see *Hot Situations, Cool Heads: How to Thrive When Conflict Arrives.* Visit *www. breakthroughskills.com* to get your copy.

- Ask questions until you're absolutely clear about the scope and timing of every element of an assignment or request: "What exactly needs to be done and when?" "How high a priority is the request?"

- Be certain everyone's expectations match: create action plans before you start work on a given project, and share these with the person who made the request or gave you the assignment.

- If you're an outside consultant or service provider, no matter how urgent a project is or how excited you are to get the order, never begin without a contract that details what you'll deliver, by when and at what cost, plus any expenses you will bill. This is a flat-out critical proactive practice for preventing unpleasant surprises on both sides of the transaction. As a bonus, insisting on a contract strengthens your reputation as a serious business with plans for long-term success.

Ask for the business

We all have an "if-only" list that looks something like this:

- "If only I hadn't said that…"
- "If only I bought that stock when it was $10 a share…"
- "If only I remembered to make that call…"
- "If only I knew then what I know now…"

Oh yes, things would sure be different today.

If you run a company or sell anything, your list might include, "If only I had just asked for the business." Ours certainly does.

Whether your sales process involves one decision maker or ten, closing a sale can seem as long and exhausting as a trans-atlantic trip in a rowboat. You meet the prospect, say hello, and do some fact-gathering. Back at the ranch, you write a great proposal, deliver it on time, follow up as promised, and then, hear…absolutely…nothing…for weeks.

You chew a few fingernails and follow up again trying to sound nonchalant.

"Jane! It's Bill. How are you/the kids/the golf game/the new program launch you were working on?"

"Great," comes the answer.

"Hey, how 'bout that proposal I sent last month? Do you think you might be interested?"

"I haven't had a chance to look at it, but I did look at your fees, and they're probably going to be too high for us."

"No problem," you expected this, "we can work that out. Just let me know your budget."

"Why don't you call me back in a week?"

"You got it. Hey, great talking to you."

You hang up and exhale for the first time in three minutes.

Jane isn't sure she remembers your name.

You call in a week (plus one day so you seem busy). You leave a voice mail, and then... more nothing.

Weeks pass, and still no deal. Afraid to push because you worry you'll lose the sale, you stay in an endless holding pattern. Frustrating, yes, but you're also not doing the prospect any favors by letting her waffle forever. She clearly needs help making a decision.

You've put yourself in the impossible position of having to react to everything the prospect is doing, never taking the reigns by simply asking for a decision: a final one, by a specific date, with a John Hancock, in ink.

Working Wisdom

Referral magic

Whether you're an independent salesperson, small business owner, or the VP of Sales for a corporation, chances are you underutilize the most important sales tool at your disposal: the referral. Compared to a cold lead, the warmth of a referral in which you can say, "I'm calling at the suggestion of our mutual friend, Jennifer Jones" puts you about five steps ahead in the sales cycle.

Why we underutilize this powerful strategy is anyone's guess. Maybe it's because we like to go after the new killer sale or fresh leads. Maybe we're uncomfortable asking clients or customers for referral names. Regardless, in our experience, every person in a sales role could and should be asking for more referrals.

Begin by speaking from your own experience:

• "I've really enjoyed working with you."

• "It's been great serving you."

• "I'm glad I was able to help you."

(continued on page 100)

(continued from page 99)

Be certain they're totally satisfied:

- *"Is this what you were looking for?"*
- *"Do you have everything you need?"*
- *"Can I help you with anything else right now?"*

Tell them you're interested in their repeat business:

- *"May I stay in touch to let you know about other products/ services that might be helpful?"*
- *"I hope we see you/I hear from you again soon."*
- *"I hope I can count on your repeat business!"*

Then explain:

- *"I've built almost my entire business on the quality of my service/product."*
- *"The vast majority of my business comes from my satisfied customers: repeat business from them and referrals to their friends and colleagues."*

Ask for referrals:

- *"Would you be willing to give me the names and contact information of a few friends or colleagues who you know would like/benefit from my product/service?"*

And be sure to get permission to use the referring customer's name when you contact the prospects.

Why is it so tough to ask for a decision? Two reasons: first, "Maybe" seems better than "No" (it isn't). And second, you haven't yet mastered the proactive practice of "asking for the business."

As you can imagine, asking for the business—essentially asking for a decision—isn't unique to sales. Every successful person, regardless of the type of work they do, has learned how to ask people to commit to a course of action. That action may have been to sign on the dotted line in a sales situation, but it could also have been to provide feedback on an idea, change a policy, or accept a meeting invitation. And it might also have been to refuse an offer.

Here are some examples of ways to "ask for the business." [One key to making this work: include a deadline. Note the words in boldface below.]:

- "I was wondering if I could have a decision from you **this week.** If not, I'll close the file for the time being."
- "By **[date]**, I'd like to know whether you're planning to move ahead. I understand you may not be prepared to make a decision by then, but that's my timeline."

- "We need to get your feedback by **[date]** in order to stay on schedule. If you wait until after that, we won't be able to make the deadline."

- "If you have no more questions for me, I'll need a decision by **[date]**."

- "I'd really like to do business with you. If you'd like to move forward with me/my company, please let me know by **[date]**."

- "I'm very interested in the position we've been talking about. If you're interested in me, I'd like to start as soon as possible. Would you please let me know **this week**?"

- "Since the meeting is next week, I need to know by **Tuesday** if you'll be there."

Your tone is critical. It's all too easy for any of these statements to sound like a demand or an ultimatum, even when that's not your intention. So be careful. Think firm, but not aggressive. Keep your voice low and calm, and add warmth that suggests, "I'm saying this because I sincerely want you to…

- …benefit from my product."

- …be at the meeting."

- …hire me for the position."

A final note on this proactive practice: in one of the more puzzling characteristics of human nature, when you take the reigns and ask for the business, you change the dynamic of the situation. As you demonstrate that you're confident that whatever you're offering—your time, expertise, product, ideas—is worthwhile, your offer becomes more, not less, desirable to your prospect. Once the prospect knows that the clock is ticking, that the offer won't stand forever, he'll be more motivated to make a decision. Again, that decision won't always be in your favor, but when it's not, it probably wouldn't have been after a three-month wait either. Better to know sooner so you can move on.

Well, that's our list, but we've barely scratched the surface. We encourage you to be on the lookout for the many other ways you can make something great happen by getting out ahead of a situation and squeezing every drop of positive potential from it.

We promised to end this section with the secret of the most potent and life-changing form of proactive thinking and action we know. We've seen it, we've used it, and we've watched it change lives.

It's called "reframing the quest."

Let's start with an example. If you wanted to improve morale on your team, which of the following do you think would set the stage for a breakthrough?

Approach 1: Chase the problem

Survey team members about the causes of low morale, asking questions like, "Why has morale on our team been steadily declining?" or "What do you think are the consequences of poor morale on our team?"

Or—

Approach 2: Reframe the quest

Ask everyone to remember when the team was at its best, functioning at the highest level and fueled by positive energy, asking questions like, "What was it like around here when morale was at its highest? What can we do to bring back that positive energy? When are we at our best as a team? What are the circumstances under which we do our best work? What can we do to recreate those circumstances?"

The questions in "Chase the problem" would help you study the situation in detail, painfully peeling away the layers of the problem one by one until you got to the root cause…aha! It's the long hours, the turnover in Payroll, excessive email, and crotchety Office Manager! Now, you're faced with the daunting task of fixing these problems (if that's even possible), with no real guarantee that doing so will improve morale. Anyway, it's likely that by the time you fix two of your four problems, new ones will already have cropped up. Such is the lot of the problem chaser!

In *The Art of Possibility* (Penguin, 2002) coauthors Rosamund Stone Zander and Benjamin Zander offer this suggestion: "Draw a different frame around the same set of circumstances and new pathways come into view. Find the right framework, and extraordinary accomplishment becomes an everyday experience."

Notice how "Reframe the quest" frames the issue in terms of the best possible outcome and puts everyone on the lookout for the steps they can take to create it. The questions in Approach 2 are also easier to answer because they're not looking to blame anyone (so no one's tempted to run for cover), they ask people to remember good times and past successes (an upbeat, fun exercise), and they get the team's mental energy flowing in a creative, constructive direction.

Legendary UCLA Basketball Coach John Wooden put this proactive principle in action every day. To prepare his players for a game, he'd tell them not to worry about the opponent. "Instead," he'd say, "just play your own game and force [the other team] to follow it...force them out of what they want to do." It would be tough not to correlate that approach to Wooden's incredible record: in twenty-seven years as head coach of UCLA, he had 620 wins and 127 losses, and won 10 NCAA championships, including seven consecutive championships from 1966 to 1973.

Drawing a different frame around a set of circumstances—in our language, "reframing the quest"—is the most powerful application of proactive thinking and action we know, one that produces breakthrough after breakthrough by putting a broader, positive, and open-ended frame around a goal *before you ever begin to pursue it*. Rather than ask, "How will we stop their offense?" Wooden reframed the team's quest: "How will we ignite our own offense?" and "How will we turn our defense into an offensive force?" In doing so, he defined brand new possibilities for his team, with record-breaking results.

Here's another example: for months, an airline's executive team, anxious to reduce the number of complaints it was receiving about lost luggage, tried different ways to fix the problem, with no results. They decided to change their approach: rather than ask, "How do we fix the lost luggage problem?" they asked, "What steps can we take to create an exceptional arrival experience for our passengers?" To begin, employees were asked to think about times they had personally enjoyed an exceptional arrival experience. Finally, success. Not only did the lost luggage problem all but disappear, passengers were treated to a superior overall arrival experience that was more efficient and pleasant, and eclipsed the competition.

The ultimate Proactive Power is...building your future, frame by frame

A few years ago, a young violinist was asked to perform for a group of inmates as part of a prison outreach program. In an open-hearted moment he accepted without really thinking it through. Sure enough, as the date drew near, he panicked about what it would be like to play for these men. Would they taunt him? Boo him off the stage? Laugh?

Though tempted to back out, he wasn't the type to welch on a commitment. He'd keep his word and perform, he decided, and with any luck, they'd tolerate him for fifteen minutes after which he'd beat a hasty retreat back home.

To his own surprise, on the day of the performance he woke up determined to overcome the fears that had almost kept him from performing. He got dressed and arrived at the prison, nerves in check and eager to share the music he so loved with these men. He took the stage, and began to play his heart out. The room grew quiet. He finished, and after a moment's silence, there was thundering applause.

Realizing he had more time and feeling at this point encouraged, he asked the group if there was a part of the concerto they might like to hear again.

Another silence.

Then, a husky voice called from the back of the room, "Yeah, could you play the part about the mother again?"

A beautiful piece of music, played with passion, transcended circumstances and touched people. But there was more happening in this story, a valuable lesson on the power of reframing a quest from something immediate and narrow and in this case, fear-based, to something broader and more positive. When the musician changed his aim from being tolerated to touching souls, his passion for the music inspired his actions and the positive result he was after began to take shape.

The secret to reframing the quest lies in the answer to a simple question:

"Regardless of what I see as problems or obstacles in this situation, what would be the ideal outcome?"

Another way to ask this question: "If I don't try to solve the problem or remove the obstacle, but instead work to create a situation in which the problem or obstacle couldn't possibly be an issue, what steps would I take?"

Some examples of how this might work in practice:

Problem: Time-sensitive information is repeatedly late.
Frame: "How do we find and fix the bottlenecks in our process?"
Reframe: "How do we create a solid, seamless process that meets or exceeds every deadline?"

Problem: An employee's performance in certain aspects of this job is lacking.
Frame: "As a manager, how can I get Joe to see the weaknesses in his performance and fix them?"
Reframe: "How do I tap Joe's strengths so he can do a superior job on every assignment and become a highly contributing member of my team?"

Problem: Customer complaints have been rising.
Frame: "How do we reduce customer complaints?"
Reframe: "How can we learn about what customers appreciate most about our service and then give them more of it?"

In each case, the reframe looks at the positive potential in the total situation, rather than the narrow band of activity needed to identify and fix the problem leaving the balance of the situation—where much more positive potential lies—untouched and untapped. The reframe trains everyone's eyes on steps they can take to create the ideal positive outcome.

Our **Take Five** activity on page 111 will help you practice this essential proactive skill.

Proactive staying power

It seems contradictory: companies say they want initiative and innovation, but they also resist change, and when it comes to risk, well, let's just say they prefer the carousel to the roller-coaster. This means that at times, your creative ideas and proactive solutions will be rejected.

How do you push past these moments and stay creative and proactive?

- Do a reality check: ask a few Trusted Colleagues whether your ideas are sound. Are you suggesting steps that are best for the larger effort and the team/client/business? If not, how can you modify your idea to make it more practical or palatable?

- Be certain your ideas are based on solid research and that you can support them with facts and data. This provides a double bonus: the more homework you do, the better able you will be to assess the risk level of your ideas, and the more intelligent and prepared you'll appear in suggesting them.

- Ask your colleagues whether your presentation style is on target. Are you presenting your ideas calmly and thoughtfully or do you sound zealous or self-promoting? Are you providing balanced information about your idea, describing both its advantages and disadvantages, as in:
  - "How much do you expect it to save (cost)?"
  - "What are the rewards (risks)?"
  - "What is the best (worst) thing that can happen?"

- Keep a finger on the pulse of the business. Does the team/client/business have an agenda or concern that may be keeping your ideas from getting through?

- Use rejection to research how you can produce a more positive result in the future. Ask directly, "Would you take a moment to explain why you disagree with me?" Find out what you might be able to do to return with a better proposal next time. This practice has an added bonus: people will often be pleasantly surprised by your honesty and genuine desire. They'll appreciate your sincere interest in their professional opinion, and may send future opportunities your way as a result.

Finally, think appreciatively: while your idea may not have been accepted, your initiative probably impressed someone. Maybe you sparked some new thinking. And, if you learned something you can apply next time, you're that much closer to having an idea accepted and implemented.

Proactive Power

Notes

_____

_____

_____

_____

_____

_____

_____

_____

_____

_____

_____

_____

_____

—— Take Five ——

Start using the Proactive Power of reframing the quest. Think of an issue that you or your team is facing right now. Frame it in terms of the problem. Then, reframe it by answering:

"If I don't try to solve the problem or remove the obstacle, but instead work to create a situation in which the problem or obstacle couldn't possibly be an issue, what steps would I take?"

Take a look again at the following examples, then, complete the table on page 113:

> **Problem:** Time-sensitive information is repeatedly late.
> **Frame:** "How do we find and fix the bottlenecks in our process?"
> **Reframe:** "How do we create a solid, seamless process that meets or exceeds every deadline?"
>
> **Problem:** An employee's performance in certain aspects of this job is lacking.
> **Frame:** "As a manager, how can I get Joe to see the weaknesses in his performance and fix them?"
> **Reframe:** "How do I tap Joe's strengths so he can do a superior job on every assignment and become a highly contributing member of my team?"

Problem: Customer complaints have been rising.

Frame: "How do we reduce customer complaints?"

Reframe: "How can we learn about what customers appreciate most about our service and then give them more of it?"

Reframing the Quest

Problem	Frame	Reframe
		"If I don't try to solve the problem or remove the obstacle, but instead work to create a situation in which the problem or obstacle couldn't possibly be an issue, what steps would I take?"

Part 3: Excuse-Free Power

Face the music...and dance

The phone was already ringing as we turned the key in the lock of the office door early one morning.

"Good morning to you!" came the way-too-chipper-for-the-hour voice on the other end.

It was Frank, a resource for an article we were writing, calling from his office in California (where it was not even 5:00 a.m.). At 92, Frank was still hard at work as an insurance salesman. He'd begun his day before dawn as he had for more than 65 years.

> "*Tomorrow is a new day. You shall begin it serenely and with too high a spirit to be encumbered with your old nonsense.*"
>
> —Ralph Waldo Emerson, American essayist, philosopher, and poet

"I'm calling to apologize," he said. "I won't be able to send the information I promised for your article until tomorrow."

"Gosh, Frank, please don't apologize."

"No, no. I promised to send it to you today, and I'm sorry."

Frank's example of gracious and full-tilt excuse-free living made such an impression on us that we still

Working Wisdom

It's just a question

In the movie Splash, after a few wedding guests innocently ask Tom Hanks who's ushering at a friend's wedding, "Where's Victoria?" Hanks bursts out, "She left me! She moved out! My life's a shambles, okay? That's the news, you want the weather? Anywhere but the first three rows!" Of course in the movie it's hilarious, but when someone reacts to a simple question this way at work, not so much.

"Is the report ready?"

"Did you talk to the customer?"

"What did you find when you looked that up?"

The questions just keep coming. Add to this the feverish pace of our work days. Mix in some sensitivities about the topic with a pinch of bad week, and it's easy to see how a simple question can feel like an attack.

Listen to this exchange we overheard recently between a systems tech and bookkeeper:

(continued on page 117)

talk about it years later. As a nonagenarian and a legendary success in his company—a millionaire many times over—he could easily have claimed to be too busy to help us, yet he was uncomfortable being late and unwilling to excuse himself from keeping his word. Frank had a reputation for treating everyone this way, keeping commitments and respecting what was important to other people—employees, clients, peers, community leaders—no matter how insignificant a particular gesture or effort was to his own success.

Refuse to excuse

Think of the true leaders you know, the ones already in positions of authority and the people who are clearly headed there. They're quick to say with an air of confidence:

- "Let me be responsible for that."
- "That happened on my watch."
- "You're absolutely right. I apologize. That should not have happened."
- "I've got it. It will be fixed this week."

We admire their strength of character with comments like: "To his credit, he didn't try to make excuses" or "She's a true leader, not one to shrink from responsibility in a tough situation." We seem to know on a gut level that people who refuse to excuse themselves and instead step in to make things right—even risking embarrassment and discomfort in the process—are the truly powerful, breakthrough-bound among us.

They've conquered what is for most of us a natural impulse: the urge to gripe. We're late for work, and we want to moan about the traffic. An idea was turned down, and we want to protest that it didn't get a fair shake. We miss a deadline, and we want to grumble about the extra week we had to wait for market data. We're asked to do work that's outside our normal scope, and we want to complain about being stretched and stressed. Our work is corrected, and we want to object…it was just fine the way it was!

Inside, we're yelling, "Hey, that's not fair! It's not my fault! And it is _not_ my responsibility!!" Oh, yes we are.

That's about to change.

(continued from page 116)

Tech: "The system can easily get disconnected from the server. If that's the problem, it's a quick fix. Do you remember if you clicked this icon on the desktop?"

Bookkeeper: "It was like that when I came in today. I did nothing to cause any kind of problem. I have never seen that icon, and I don't know what you're talking about."

Tech: "Um, okay. Let me try something here."

Bookkeeper: "You can try whatever you want, but I did nothing different from what I do every day."

Tech: "Okay, there you go. Should be fine now. Want me to show you what I did?"

Bookkeeper: "I don't need you to show me how to fix a mistake I didn't make."

It was embarrassing to be sitting within earshot of this conversation, and of course we knew nothing about the background of the situation or the history of this relationship. Still, from where we were sitting, "Did you click this icon?" was just a question, not a live grenade.

No matter what kind of day you're having, what mistake you've made, or what's at

(continued on page 118)

(continued from page 117)

stake, it's still just a question. Answering defensively or with a attack is a counterproductive response that says more than you want it to. And this is true even when the question is intended to grill you. Treat it like just a question, and you stay in control of the situation, and communicate command over the topic.

If for some reason, you're not ready to answer, buy yourself time by saying, "Great question...

- *...I'm not sure. Let me give that some thought."*

- *...I need to look that up."*

- *...I'd like to call Susan in accounting first."*

If you're on the phone, you can even put the caller on hold, take a breath to collect yourself and get back on the line with a calm answer.

How powerful do you want to be?

Ever risk life and limb by working with someone who's always on the defensive or full of excuses? And while you may know that the person's behavior stems from low self-esteem, personal problems, a harsh internal critic, or even a history of working for monster managers, none of that helps you when you're hit full on with a defensive outburst.

If you have to give feedback to someone entrenched in this work style, you feel the impulse to say it super-fast and then quickly run for cover. No matter how carefully you word it, or how helpful your tone, the person hears the feedback as an attack and responds with swift defensive maneuvers:

- "That's because you told me to..."

- "I told you at the beginning I wouldn't be able to..."

- "They always do this when I ask them to..."

- "It's totally unfair that I have to..."

- "Sure, that's fine for other people, but you can't expect me to..."

Can there be anything more tedious?

Though this is the extreme, it's easy to drift into the habit of excuse making unaware that it's even happening. A problem will surface when you least expect it. You'll say or do something you later regret. A client will catch you off-guard with a question you haven't the vaguest idea how to answer. Slowly, the thought will start to take shape in the back of your mind, "That's because he..." or "I would have, but..." or "I can't be expected to know..."

Whatever you do, don't let that excuse make the trip from your mind to your mouth, no matter how right you are. Excuse making isn't practical, it robs you of your power, and it says more about you than you realize...none of it positive:

"You're right!"

The moment you start to rationalize your behavior, giving your reasons why you did what you did, you may as well stand on a platform and yell, "You're right!" Your reaction says that you agree you did something wrong, something that needs to be explained and excused. However, instead of excusing you, your reasons do just the opposite: they validate what you're being blamed for because they say the

Working Wisdom

Excuses, excuses

Note a few important differences between an excuse and an explanation. Explanations spark forward-thinking ideas and positive action. Excuses are disempowering and even disabling; they stop or slow progress. Explanations are group- or team-oriented. Excuses are usually self-centered, aimed at protecting oneself.

Excuses are rationalizations that sound passive, and often include blaming:

> *"We would have started on time, but our workload was too great. Then, Marketing gave us the wrong information. I left Tom a voice mail about the problem, but I'm still waiting to hear from him. I'll let you know when he gets back to me."*

Explanations are fact-based and emphasize personal responsibility and corrective action, without placing blame on people or circumstances:

> *"Our timeline was shorter than we would have liked. Also, some of the*

(continued on page 120)

(continued from page 119)

data we used to build our models was incomplete. My sincere apologies. We'll go back now and redo the calculations with the full data. We'll have them to you by tomorrow."

Pause here and read these two examples aloud, and when you do, notice how much stronger the explanation sounds, how commanding, future-focused, and action-oriented: the speaker carefully avoids placing blame, provides a brief explanation (short timeline, incomplete data), quickly apologizes, and then commits to a specific, time-bound remedy.

The excuse is passive: the person "would have" gotten started on time, left a voice mail (instead of finding the person), and is "waiting" to hear back.

accusation is worth your time and attention. And when the accusation is untrue or inaccurate, you give your accuser incredible power over your time, mood, confidence level, and reputation. A skilled investigator will even interpret someone's denial, especially a detailed denial, as a sign of culpability. The more the person says, the guiltier they appear, and the more the investigator will probe.

"They're wrong!"

In the heat of the moment, offloading responsibility by blaming someone or something else (and blame is a form of excuse making) definitely gives you relief from embarrassment or discomfort. But the relief is fleeting. Though it's tempting to think you're helping yourself by pointing a finger at someone else, it just doesn't work that way. The minute you begin to blame someone or something else, you give up your power to make a difference in the situation. If *they* are responsible, then *they* need to fix it, and *you* will end up accepting a solution that may not be in your best interest. You've lost control of the outcome.

"I'm right, right?"

A client of ours has this comic strip framed in the office at the back of her store:

A person slowly stands up from behind a desk and declares, frame by frame:

"That's it! I'm not going to stay in this crummy job forever."

"I've got big dreams! Big hopes! Big plans! I'm going to take action!"

"Starting TODAY!"

"I'M FINALLY TAKING CHARGE OF MY LIFE!"

And then in the final frame, the figure droops, hangs its head, and says,

"Okay?"

Yeah, it's funny. But it also does a good job of capturing another subtle quality of excuse making that robs us of power: approval seeking. In trying to justify your actions, reactions, choices, and job description with lots of detailed information on who, what, when, where, why, and how, you're in effect saying, "You agree with me, right? I mean I'm right, right? Because I'm only actually right if you say I am." As you work overtime to explain and justify your actions, you create the impression that you won't proceed until the listener approves. It's as if you're hoping to shift ultimate responsibility away from yourself and onto the listener. "If he says it's a good idea, then I've got an instant escape hatch: I can blame him if it doesn't go well." It's a little like making the other person pick the movie or the restaurant so they'll be responsible if it isn't any good.

"Don't trust me. I'm rarely right."

A habit of excuse making can steal your credibility. It doesn't take long for the people in your work life to pick up on an excuse-making vibe. Worst case, they may start to think, "I'm not even going to bother asking Bill. I'm not going to get a straight answer from him anyway, just a bunch of excuses." Lose your credibility, and you lose your voice. The title of a great book by communications expert Bert Decker says it all: *You've Got to be Believed to be Heard* (St. Martin's Press, 2007).

In addition to being at the heart of every strong relationship and breakthrough in the making, the words, "I trust you" are high on the list of life's greatest compliments. Earning that is tough. Losing it is far too easy. Don't let a habit of excuse making rob you of this critical career and business-building asset.

So how powerful do you want to be? Never mind money, position, or influence over people. Those are fleeting: promotion last month, pink slip today. Disposable income last year, coupon clipping this year. We're talking about something much more durable and valuable: personal power. Strength of character. Resourcefulness. Confidence that you'll make it through every situation your career or business throws at you.

Powerful people don't let themselves make excuses. They don't place blame. And neither one of these characteristics is an accident. They deliberately refuse to rationalize their actions or offload responsibility because they want to be in command of the situation and free to create a solution that works for them.

Your turn

Conquering excuse making—cutting it out of your life completely—is just a matter of habit, really. Like optimism, it starts as a conscious choice. In time, choice becomes habit, and habit becomes a standard of excellence so ingrained in your actions that you can't remember operating any other way. You reach a point where the only impulse you feel is to get all the facts of the situation, figure out the resources you've got to address it, take positive action, and move on.

Let's take a look now at some practical strategies for staying excuse-free:

When you're accused of something (deservedly or not):

1. Mentally take responsibility.

2. Apologize and thank the person for bringing the issue to your attention.

3. End with a remedy.

Let's take these one at a time:

Mentally take responsibility.

"Are you serious?" we hear you shout. "*Take* responsibility? What if I'm not in the wrong?" We're not saying be a doormat, nor for a moment are we suggesting that you allow yourself to be blamed (or blame yourself) for circumstances that you didn't create or those outside your control.

Rather than blame, we're challenging you to take (maybe even seize) response-ability, the ability to respond to tough situations constructively.

This is an *internal* step; it takes place only in your mind. There's no verbal, "Yes, I did it" or "Yes, I'm to blame" along with it. Seizing response-ability is a personal choice to unleash your inventive powers and start generating some forward-looking solutions. Think of it this way: the person who takes response-ability for a situation also takes command of it. Response-ability gives you the power to design a solution that creates the best possible result...and to enjoy the recognition that goes along with it.

Apologize and thank the person for bringing the issue to your attention.

Next, another challenge: the (ahem) apology.

Here's what it sounds like:

Colleague, client, or customer:

- "I'd like to know why you _____."
- "Didn't you say that _____? What happened?"
- "I thought we agreed _____. Why didn't you do that?"
- "I never said you should _____. Why did you do that?"

You:

- "I'm sorry that happened. I didn't realize you felt that was important."
- "You're absolutely right, that does need to be fixed. Thanks for letting me know. I appreciate your honesty."
- "I'm sorry you feel that way. I'm glad we have the kind of relationship where you can be so open with me."

In each example, notice three things: 1) the apology is brief, 2) the latter part of the statement begins to shift the focus away from you, and 3) you're not apologizing for what you did, but rather for the situation—a subtle but important difference. You're saying you're sorry the situation arose or you're sorry someone is upset. The difference is significant: when you apologize for the situation, you're actually conveying that you're in command of it. You're not trying to defend yourself or wiggle out of responsibility, but rather preventing a blaming or excuse-making discussion, taking control, and moving the conversation on to a remedy with a positive future focus.

"How can that make any sense?" you may think. "By apologizing, aren't I admitting it's my fault?" Great question. This is where your must pay careful attention to your tone and body language. The key is to speak from a position of strength and personal command, not teeth-gritting anger or head-hanging subservience. Your apology must be sincere and honest; whether or not you think they should, someone feels wronged. And while that person may not directly influence your success, he or she may know someone who does.

The moment you apologize without defending yourself and then immediately look forward and suggest solutions, you bring a blast of power and positive potential to the situation by:

- Changing the mood, maybe throwing some cool water on a smoldering fire.

- Preventing the situation from escalating into a relationship-straining mess.

- Building a bridge to the other person by validating his or her concerns without demeaning yourself.

- Shifting the focus of the situation away from the problem and toward the solution.

End with a remedy.

Finally, suggest a solution:

You:

- "I'll have that fixed for you by tomorrow."

- "By Tuesday, I will _____..."

- "This won't happen again."

- "Let's talk about how we can _____ in the future."

Provide as much detail as possible (action steps, timing, etc.) and keep your promises!

If you had to estimate the amount of energy you should spend on each of these three steps in a given situation, it would look something like this:

1. Mentally take responsibility. (20 percent)

2. Apologize and thank the person for bringing the issue to your attention. (5 percent)

3. End with a remedy. (75 percent)

Take command of the situation by taking response-ability. Then, after a quick apology, spend your best energy building a solution.

A fact-based explanation

What if, because of the nature of the situation or the position of the person leveling the complaint—a client who's given you a large contract, someone very senior to you in the organization, a Key Influencer who went out on a limb to recommend you—you must provide an explanation? Some strategies for doing so while staying powerfully excuse-free:

- Try to limit your reasons to three: a large enough number to satisfy the other person, a small enough number not to belabor the point.

- If you can, avoid putting your reasons in writing or in an email. Email tends to be too sharp and quick, and it lacks tone. Putting your reasons in writing also creates a permanent record of the situation, and you don't have control over where that record will be forwarded or how it might be used.

- Ask to meet with the person so that you can give the situation the importance and active, two-way dialogue it deserves. Having this conversation in person also gives you more control of the mood and the outcome because you can watch the person's nonverbal cues, respond directly in real time to his or her reactions, and build rapport.

- Keep your reasons simple and fact-based, not blame-based. Focus on issues, not people.

- Move the conversation toward a specific time-bound remedy as quickly as possible.

Excuse-Free Power

Notes

_____

_____

_____

_____

_____

_____

_____

_____

_____

_____

_____

_____

_____

_____

_____

How to Build a Breakthrough

Step 1:   Congratulate yourself! You're ready to take action.

Step 2:   Take a few minutes to recall your best achievements from the past year. Remind yourself how talented and valuable you are.

Step 3:   Build momentum slowly:

- Each time you tackle a new Breakthrough Skill, test drive one or two of our ideas each week rather than try to use every suggestion right away.

- Find small, low-risk experiences—including experiences outside work (church, family, community service)—to try new skills. For example, to strengthen presentation skills, volunteer to make small presentations at work to just a few people, lead a committee at your church, or join Toastmasters. To improve self-promotion skills, prepare a 30-second self introduction, then go to an industry or professional association meeting and introduce yourself to at least two people.

- As your momentum builds, push harder: deliberately create more significant and visible opportunities to strengthen the skill you're working on.

Step 4:   Be sure your closest colleagues know about the skill you're working to improve. Ask for their support and feedback on your progress.

Step 5:   Recognize and celebrate even the smallest successes. Each one is a victory!

Step 6:   Use a *Breakthrough Journal©* (available at *www. breakthroughskills.com*) to record your achievements and the steps you'll take to showcase them to the people who influence your success.

BREAKTHROUGH
skills.com

Dear Reader,

Being positive, proactive, and excuse-free won't guarantee you success, but it will let you face every day with optimism, your head full of ideas and sky-high possibilities, your actions focused and purposeful. Your work life will have new energy, and you'll look to the future with more confidence.

So step out of the box with a bang—and never, ever look back.

We wish you blue skies and breakthroughs,

Doug and Diana

For a more excellent resources on High Possibility Thinking, please visit us at *www.breakthroughskills.com.*

260 Columbia Avenue, Suite 5, Fort Lee, NJ 07024
877-312-5400 • 201-224-3800
info@breakthroughskills.com • www.breakthroughskills.com

Care to Share?

What did you think of *Step Out of the Box With a Bang?*
Did it help you? How? What changes should we make
to future editions? If you care to share, please visit us
at www.breakthroughskills.com and write a review.

Thank you!

BREAKTHROUGH
skills.com

Please enjoy this sneak peek at our book
*The THINK! Workbook, A Guided Brainstorm
to the Future of Your Life's Work.* To get your
copy, visit us at www.breakthroughskills.com.

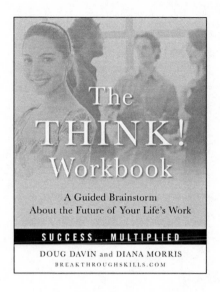

Let's Go!

Nothing compares to the air on a mountain above tree line. If you're a hiker, you know what we mean. If not, picture aching legs, sore from lifting you thousands of feet over rocks, roots, and branches, through mud and streams. You've probably tripped a few times and been whipped in the face by a branch or two. For hours, maybe days, you've been climbing, staring at tree after tree.

But at some point, the trees began to thin out and get shorter until suddenly, they were gone. Stepping up into the clearing, you stop.

There's a quiet so deep you clear your throat just to be sure you haven't lost your hearing. Below, you can see how far you've come. Around you, neighboring peaks are visible. Beyond them, the range. Then, the horizon.

The summit may or may not be in view, but you know it's there, and it's closer than before. You know too that every sweaty, heart-pounding step you've taken to get here has been absolutely necessary. After all that time in the trees, you finally have your bearings.

And the air...clean, fresh, head-clearing crisp.

Above tree line, there is a pause. And with it, quiet, fresh air, perspective. The climb has been tough, but the view is spectacular.

Are you engaged?

What makes you wake up without an alarm clock? Rush out of the shower searching for a pen to write down an idea? Get so engaged in your work that you forget to eat lunch?

Some people immediately point to the content of their work: "I can edit/paint/cook/draw blueprints for hours on end and not feel tired."

Others say things like...

- "New projects, new people, travel...all the time. I can't stand routine."
- "Hyper-challenge. I like building teams or businesses from scratch, turning bad or even seemingly hopeless situations around. But once I get there, I'm itching for the next 'impossible' goal."

- "It doesn't sound ambitious, but I like routine and a predictable schedule in my job. I love knowing exactly what's expected of me...what I have to do to be recognized and succeed."

- "Working with a team that's so tight that we spend time together, even outside of the office."

- "Organizing! Making an office or a team run on all cylinders and really hum with efficiency."

- "An atmosphere of respect and concern for the company's employees and customers."

- "A must-achieve goal, especially as I get closer to reaching it."

- "Being able to hang up the phone, knowing I really helped someone is what makes work worthwhile. It sounds corny, but sometimes that actually gives me goosebumps."

- "The freedom of sales. Selling keeps me out in front, not behind the scenes. I would die sitting in an office all day."

Set these comments in a saucepan and let them simmer for a while. When all else boils away, what's left? For the people who say things like: "I've got to matter to the people I serve" or "I've got to enjoy the people I work with," relationships are paramount. It's as if they're saying, "I do my best work when my business relationships are strong and positive."

For people who say, "I need freedom and flexibility" and "I need structure, routine, and predictability," the structure of their days is their principal concern.

People who say things like, "I've got to believe in the company" and "I've got to know the company believes in me" are saying, "The culture and atmosphere of the company I work for really matter to me."

People looking for "hyper-challenge" and exhilarating goals thrive on the thrill of the chase.

What about you? What gets you so engrossed in your work that you lose track of time? When, where, and how do you do your best work? Before you just shrug your shoulders and go back to work...

Hit the *Pause* button!

If you're like us, you spend your days running from task to task, answering calls and emails, fixing problems, handling whatever comes your way.

And with your best energy focused on the tasks that scream the loudest and demand attention, the important tasks—the meetings, phone calls, and new projects that could help you make real progress—get put on hold.

When someone asks you what you want out of your work, your natural response is something like "I don't have time to stare at my navel! I've got too much work to do!"

If you live in this mode, you know just how draining it is, but there's a greater cost: all that adrenaline and momentum keep you running in the trees, unable to get your bearings and figure out if you're headed in the right direction. A client once bottom lined it for us this way: "The trouble is, there's no time to think! I just run from meeting to meeting and deadline to deadline. I'm keeping up with what I've got to do, but not making any real progress. Then again, I can't really say that...because I've had no time to actually think about it!"

One day, though, something <u>will</u> stop you.

You'll be passed over for a promotion, or a plum opportunity will be given to a colleague rather than to you. You'll lose a key account or a critical sale. There may be a job loss or serious illness in your family. Maybe more positively, you'll be promoted and take on lots more responsibility, your business will win an account that stretches its resources a little too thin, or your company will be acquired and you'll face new challenges with new people.

And you'll begin, finally, to do something you've never done before—

Stop and think...*really* think:

- "I worked so hard to make this business profitable. Now that it is, I'm not excited about it any more. Maybe it was just the superhuman climb out of the red that energized me."

- "I thought I'd be more upset about being fired, but for some weird reason, I'm relieved. Now what do I do?"

- "For the first time, I'm responsible for other people. I never managed employees before, and honestly, I don't feel ready for it."

- "I've been hoping for that VP position for two years. Now that Carolyn got it instead of me, I'm stuck. There's nowhere for me to progress here. I need a new plan."

- "If I never spent another day forecasting inventory, would I really miss it?"

- "I've accomplished a lot in my sales career, exceeded every goal I had for myself. I just have no idea what's next."

What about you? What type of work do you find truly exciting and lose-track-of-time engaging? And what's next for you? Your options and decision-making power increase tenfold when you answer these questions <u>before</u> circumstances force you to.

The THINK! Workbook is your *Pause* button. It's a "guided brainstorm" of questions and exercises designed to make you stop long enough to identify your signature strengths and professional values and think about where these match the work you do today…and where they don't. *THINK!* will also help you write a personal definition of success, including your must-achieve goals, and create a list of the people (your Trusted Colleagues, Mentors, and Key Influencers) who can help you reach them.

Unlike other New Heights resources which zero-in on one breakthrough skill, *THINK!* helps you focus on all the Breakthrough Skills at once:

1. **Conflict Management:** *Keep cool in hot situations*

2. **Confident Communication:** *Sharpen your writing and presentations*

3. **Active Listening:** *Hear the possibilities*

4. **High Possibility Thinking:** *Set great expectations*

5. **Leadership and Teambuilding:** *Unify and motivate your team*

6. **Practical Persuasion:** *Create the win-win*

7. **Skillful Self Promotion:** *Boost your reputation for excellence*

Right now

It's time to get some perspective and focus your thinking. Savor the amazing things you've already accomplished, and listen as you remind yourself of who you are, what you value, and what you want to offer yourself and the world.

So, make a pot of coffee, sharpen your pencil, find a comfortable chair in a quiet spot, and come *THINK!* with us.

—Doug and Diana

Important!

Our goal in offering this guided brainstorm is not to encourage you to make a career move or a radical change in your business. The goal is the title: THINK! We simply want to help you open your mind and eyes to a broad, high potential vision of your future, one filled with prosperity in all its forms: enrichment, growth, satisfaction, and contribution.

Clients tell us that THINK! helped make them more aware of the professional and person they aspire to become. Ideally, THINK! will do the same for you, leaving you with fresh insights about your potential and the possibilities for your career or business.

Part 1: My Greatest Achievements:

Uncover Your "Signature Strengths"

How to

In his book, *Authentic Happiness* (Free Press, 2002), Dr. Martin Seligman, Chairman of the University of Pennsylvania's Positive Psychology Center, talks about a strategy for creating a happy life. Based on Aristotle's philosophy of what constitutes "the good life," Seligman suggests that happiness requires knowing your "signature strengths" and using them as often as possible.

Signature strengths…what a great phrase! You could call them your unique assets, natural gifts or skills sharpened through experience.

What are your signature strengths? A great way to answer this question is to take a close look at your greatest achievements. In this first section of *The THINK! Workbook*, we want you to shine a bright light on these peak moments in your career. What steps did you take to create these achievements? Where were you? Who supported you? How did you involve these people? How did the conversation go? How did you feel? What does all this tell you about where your signature strengths lie?

> "One does not discover new lands without consenting to lose sight of the shore for a very long time."
>
> —Andre Gide,
> French author,
> Winner of the
> Nobel Prize in literature

These successes are a goldmine of information about your power and potential, and this important first step will help you zero-in on them, mine them for evidence of your strengths, and then use this information to create more success for yourself, your team, and your company in the future.

These successes are a goldmine of information about your power and potential. And this important first step will help you zero-in on them, mine them for evidence of your strengths, and then use this powerful information to create more success for yourself, your team, and your company in the future.

Now you...

Take some time now to remember your greatest achievements from the past few years (for example: a significant project you completed, a challenging sale you closed, a successful product/service you launched, a team you built or strengthened, a new relationship you established, or a rocky relationship you put on firmer footing).

THINK! It Through

Answer the following in writing below. Use extra paper if needed:

1. List two of your greatest achievements from the last three years, when you were at your best, delivering the highest value to your team and/or company.

2. Who else was involved? How did the conversation go? How did you feel?

3. What is the story behind each success? What steps did you take? Was anything about your approach new or different each time?

4. How did you know you were successful? What was the single most positive piece of feedback you received about each achievement?

5. What do these successes tell you about the circumstances (relationships, working atmosphere, job content, type of challenge) under which you do your best work?

6. What do your greatest achievements say about the "signature strengths" you bring to your job, team, and/ or business? What have others told you are your greatest strengths? Does your view and theirs match?

Jumpstart

Starting today, each time you have a victory at work, take some time not just to celebrate, but to brainstorm. Ask yourself what we call **The Great Questions**:

1. "What did I do right? What steps can I take to repeat this success consistently?"

2. "What other projects or tasks can I apply these steps to?"

3. "How did I rely on my key relationships…who helped me and how?"

4. "How can I be sure the influential people in my business life know about this achievement?"

5. "What does this success tell me about my strengths?"

Go to *www. breakthroughskills. com* for a free, printable version of The Great Questions you can post in your work space.

You're Never Alone

In every Breakthrough Skills resource, from our books to our coaching sessions to our Telesession calls, we stress the importance of building relationships with people we call your Success Partners:

1. **Trusted Colleagues** are your professional friends, usually peers, you can easily talk to and brainstorm with. They almost always have time for you and give you objective, realistic feedback while keeping your best interests at heart.

2. **Mentors** are people whose success you admire and would like to emulate. Mentors are role models whose support and advice prevent you from having to "reinvent the wheel" and save you from making the mistakes they made.

3. **Key Influencers** are your gatekeepers. They are the people in your work life—peers, colleagues, clients, leaders—who can open doors for you: introducing you to key people, spotlighting your skills or accomplishments at key moments, or "pulling strings" to send solid opportunities your way.

Rely on your Success Partners. Ask for their help. Use them as honesty springboards, accountability partners, and personal sages as you reach for new heights in your career or business. And whenever you have the chance, do the same for them.

Disclaimer

All our products and services aim to help you open your mind and eyes to a broad, high potential vision of your future and build the career or business breakthrough you're after. Your results, however, are your responsibility. Breakthroughskills.com and New Heights Media do not guarantee the results obtained by the users of its Rapid-Read Handbooks™, BTS QuickTools™, Breakthrough Coaching, Workshops, or Telesessions.